THE FOUR
INSIGHTS

Also by Alberto Villoldo, Ph.D.

Dance of the Four Winds (with Erik Jendresen)

The First Story Ever Told (with Erik Jendresen)

The Four Winds (with Erik Jendresen)

Healing States (with Stanley Krippner, Ph.D.)

Island of the Sun (with Erik Jendresen)

*Mending the Past and Healing the Future with Soul Retrieval**

Millennium Glimpses into the 21st Century

The Realms of Healing (with Stanley Krippner, Ph.D.)

Shaman, Healer, Sage

Yoga, Power, and Spirit (available April 2007)*

*Available from Hay House

THE FOUR
INSIGHTS

Wisdom, Power, and Grace
of the Earthkeepers

ALBERTO VILLOLDO, Ph.D.

HAY HOUSE, INC.
Carlsbad, California
London • Sydney • Johannesburg
Vancouver • Hong Kong • New Delhi

Published and distributed in the United States by: Hay House, Inc. •
Published and distributed in Australia by: Hay House Australia Pty. Ltd.
• *Published and distributed in the United Kingdom by:* Hay House UK,
Ltd. • *Published and distributed in the Republic of South Africa by:* Hay
House SA (Pty), Ltd. • *Distributed in Canada by:* Raincoast • *Published
in India by:* Hay House Publications (India) Pvt. Ltd. • *Distributed in
India by:* Media Star

Editorial supervision: Jill Kramer • *Design:* Tricia Breidenthal

ISBN: 978-1-4019-1045-7

Printed in the United States of America

For Stanley Krippner, teacher,
mentor, and friend; and don Antonio,
Laika and son of the sun.

CONTENTS

INTRODUCTION

The Way of the Earthkeepers

For millennia, secret societies of Native American medicine men and women carefully guarded their wisdom teachings and acted as stewards of nature. These "Earthkeepers" existed in many nations and were called several different names; for example, in the Andes and the Amazon they were known as the "Laika."

In 1950, a group of Laika from high in the Andes traveled to an annual gathering of shamans that occurred at the foot of one of the holy mountains. The local natives looked at the ponchos the Laika were wearing and instantly recognized the markings of the high-shaman priests. They realized that this was a group of medicine men and women thought to have vanished after the time of the Conquest. These high-shamans, knowing that humankind was on the verge of a huge upheaval, had finally come out of seclusion to offer all people the wisdom that would sustain us through the great changes we were about to face, which would help us alter our reality and give birth to a better world.

Conquistadors and Cover-ups

The Earthkeepers teach that all of creation—the earth, humans, whales, rocks, and even the stars—is made of vibration and light. Nothing we perceive as material and real exists, other than as a dream that we're projecting onto the world. This dream is a story, and we believe it to be real . . . even though it isn't. Earthkeeper practices and wisdom teach us how to rewrite our stories about our lives, to do what the shamans call "dreaming the world into being."

These invaluable teachings, known as *the four insights,* were kept under wraps for a very good reason. With the arrival of the conquistadors (the European pilgrims and immigrants who first looted and plundered and then set-tled the Americas), the Laika were relentlessly persecuted. Many, particularly the women, were branded witches and sorcerers; and they were imprisoned, tortured, and killed. Their knowledge was considered so dangerous and threat-ening to the Catholic Church that even now, 200 years after the Spanish Inquisition shut down everywhere else in the world, the Church continues to keep an office active in Lima, Peru. The Office for the Extirpation of Idolatries is run by the Dominican Order, who, in the 15th century, declared Joan of Arc a heretic and sentenced her to death by burning at the stake.

The Laika realized that this knowledge about human beings' capacity to manifest our dreams is tremendously powerful and could be easily abused by those lacking eth-ics. Thus, they concealed the knowledge not only from the conquistadors, but even from most of their fellow indigenous peoples. Nevertheless, they recognized that the four insights belong to all—so when the Laika met a white person who didn't possess the arrogant, hostile mind-set of the conqueror, they were willing to share their wisdom teachings. Shortly after the Conquest, for instance, they took into their fold a Catholic priest, a Jesuit by the name of Father Blas Valera, who also happened to be a *mestizo* (half Indian and half Spanish).

Father Valera became initiated into the mysteries of the Laika and wrote four books about their teachings, but unfortunately, three of these tomes mysteriously disappeared during the Inquisition (the fourth remains in a private collection in Italy). Valera claimed that the Inka were as civilized as the Europeans because the Inka were able to write by using a complex system of colored strings with knots tied in them known as *Quipus*. When Valera's order discovered what he was up to, they incarcerated him for six years until his death. Why did the Jesuits silence one of their own priests? Why were they so afraid of the wisdom he was recording for the benefit of all? And why did they forbid the ordination of any more mestizo or indigenous priests after Valera was defrocked?

I was another non-Indian taken into the fold of the Laika, initiated into the lineage of the Wisdomkeepers in the Amazon near the Inka city of Cusco. Yet it was never my intention to become part of this lineage—as a medical anthropologist, I was only interested in studying the healing practices of the shamans. As fortune or destiny would have it, I ended up meeting my mentor, don Antonio. He was one of the last of the living Laika, and he took me under his wing and trained me for nearly 25 years. He was a man of many lives—during the day, he was a university professor; in the evenings, a master medicine man. He was born in a high mountain village and worked with the tools and practices of the 15th century, yet he was conversant in the ways of the 21st. Although he was a descendant of the Inka, he would tell me that the Laika are much older than the Inka, whose culture was masculine and militaristic. The Laika's teachings were from an earlier time, when the feminine aspect of the divine was recognized. I once told him that I felt lucky to have found him, and he said, "What makes you think you found me, if the Church could not find us for the last 500 years?"

This book is the result of the seed that don Antonio planted in me—and now, as an Earthkeeper myself, I share a major shift with you that was predicted by the ancients, in order to help you prepare for the time of evolution we're now entering.

Homo Luminous

According to the prophecies of the Maya, the Hopi, and the Inka, we're at a turning point in human history. The Maya identified the year 2012 as the culmination of a period of great turmoil and upheaval, one in which a new species of human will give birth to itself. We're going to take a quantum leap into what we are becoming, moving from *Homo sapiens* to *Homo luminous*—that is, beings with the ability to perceive the vibration and light that make up the physical world at a much higher level. For the first time, all of humanity will be able to evolve not *between* generations but *within* a generation, which contradicts our beliefs about how evolution works. We'll take a biological quantum leap within our own lifetimes; and the physical, emotional, and spiritual traits we acquire will be passed on to our children and our children's children.

If this sounds hard to believe, consider that you create a new copy of your body about every eight months, as your cells replace themselves. By following the four insights contained within this book and implementing their practices, you can manifest a physical body that's free of the tyranny of the genes you inherited from your parents and the medical maladies they bring you. But even more important, you can unchain yourself from the limiting emotional and spiritual stories you've inherited or bought into over the course of your life.

Thanks to the discoveries of quantum physics, we've come to understand that all matter is densely packed light. But the Laika have known about the luminous nature of reality for millennia—they know that vibration and light can organize themselves into a thousand shapes and forms. First, there is a luminous matrix, and then this blueprint gives birth to life. Vibration and light swirl and condense around the luminous matrix and give birth to a whale, for instance, and then whales can give birth to other whales.

The human body also has a luminous matrix: We're enveloped by a luminous energy field (LEF) that manifests the form and health of the body. The LEF organizes the body in the same way that the energy fields of a magnet arrange iron filings on top of a piece of glass. Just as with the example of the whales, humans can give birth to other humans, but a new kind of human has to come from a new luminous matrix. Over millennia, the Laika learned to access the biological blueprint of light and assist Spirit in the unfolding of creation. They also learned how to heal disease and create extraordinary states of health, as well as to craft and shape their personal destinies, by changing the LEF.

We can think of the LEF as the software that gives instructions to DNA, which is the hardware that manufactures the body. Mastery of the insights lets us access the latest version of the software and allows each of us to create a new body that ages, heals, and dies differently. Without the ability to reprogram the LEF, we're trapped in the stories we inherited; that is, we age, heal, live, and die the way our parents and grandparents did, reliving their physical ills and emotional ailments. The four insights contained in these pages allow us to break free of the tyranny of our familial curses, the stories that haunted our ancestors.

Mastery of the insights even allowed the Laika to create new life on Earth—to bring forth a new species of butterfly in the Amazon, for example. It allowed them to move gigantic boulders up the sides of mountains, as was required to build the Inka cities in the clouds. The Bible tells us that our faith can move mountains, but we've forgotten that we have the ability to do so. The insights teach us that the first mountain we must move is the one that blocks our perception of our own luminous nature.

In becoming *Homo luminous,* we'll give up the ways of the conquistador and discard the masculine theology that values command, control, and dominion over nature, a theology that justifies the exploitation of the earth's rivers and forests because they're seen merely as resources for human consumption. Instead, we'll embrace an older mythology that has become lost to most humans, a feminine theology of cooperation and sustainability.

Reclaiming the Feminine Aspect of the Divine

And God blessed them, and God said unto them, Be fruitful, and multiply, and replenish the earth, and subdue it: and have dominion over the fish of the sea, and over the fowl of the air, and over every living thing that moveth upon the earth.
— Genesis 1:28

In religious traditions that embrace a masculine divinity, the divine is seen as a force that resides in the heavens, far away from us. In the West, we have come to believe that to be close to God, we have to work hard at our relationship with Him, praying and sacrificing. We feel that we must earn the love and attention of our Creator, Who threw us out of paradise for daring to eat from the tree of knowledge of good and evil. According to the ancient story, we were supposed to remain like children, so in tasting the fruit that God had forbidden us, we showed our independence, roused His wrath, and doomed ourselves to living a life of hard work and misery, alleviated only by God's grace.

However, in the more ancient, feminine theologies, we were never expelled from the garden or separated from God. (For example, the Australian Aborigines weren't kicked out of Eden, and neither were the sub-Saharan Africans or the Native Americans.) Instead, we were given the garden in order to be its stewards and caretakers. According to these older beliefs, the divine puts Her life force into the seeds that we plant in the rich, fertile earth. We express that potential, expanding with divinity as we bear the fruit that feeds all of humanity. The Laika, who embrace that old, feminine theology, would say, "We are here not only to grow corn but to grow gods." In other words, we actually participate with the divine in the co-creation of our universe. We recognize that everything in our world is sacred, including us, and that our job is to foster the fullest expression of that divinity.

A Theology Made Manifest

Over the course of history, these two very different theologies have had very different effects on how human beings have interacted with each other and our world. For example, when the Europeans arrived in the Americas, they believed that they had found a vast, unpopulated land with crystalline rivers and abundant game, and that God had provided this bounty for them to use as they saw fit. In truth, more than 100 million native people occupied this land, living in balance with their environment. The natives embraced feminine theologies and trusted that as long as they lived in harmony with the earth, the Great Mother would provide for them.

The first settlers of the Americas had never been afraid to travel long distances—from Asia into North America, and ultimately, South America—because they believed that wherever they went, there would be ample food and shelter. So they hunted and gathered and learned to cultivate crops. The Earthkeepers brought this wisdom with them as they made their great trek across the Bering Strait thousands of years ago and settled the Americas, from the northernmost tip of Alaska to that of Patagonia. Their wisdom originated in sanctuaries high in the Himalayas and was brought to the Americas by the audacious travelers.

When masculine theologies began to appear as villages grew into cities, a new mentality started to dominate. Rather than work with the resources available to them, people began to attack their neighbors in the hope of acquiring more land and wealth. No longer were they willing to settle for enough to sustain them; rather, greed began to predominate. They believed that all the food in the world belonged to them, that they were at the top of the food chain instead of the *stewards* of the food chain.

In Europe, these ideas arrived with the Indo-European peoples from central Asia 6,000 years ago. They believed that they had divine justification for their invasions and conquests (in fact, the swords they used to vanquish others would later be turned upside down to become the cross, which was a symbol of the Crusades). The invaders felt that they had a sacred right to resources because they worshipped the "proper" God, and even claimed that they were honoring their Creator by slaying the enemy infidels who wouldn't convert to their belief system.

The Europeans improved the technology of warfare so much that by the time Francisco Pizarro and Hernán Cortés arrived in the New World in the 16th century, they were able to bring down the Aztec and Inka empires with fewer than 400 men, equipped with guns, steel, horses . . . and germs. The Laika fled to the mountains, where they kept the old feminine theology safely hidden, knowing that someday they'd need to come down to the valleys and remind the people of the ancient, sustainable way of living.

We see the devastating results of this masculine mythology played out today. Our world is being rapidly deforested, our waters polluted, our air contaminated, and our topsoil eroded. Our weather is changing because of global warming, and as a result, African droughts have worsened; hurricanes are more fierce; and each year, 100 to 1,000 times more species of plants and animals are disappearing from the earth than they did 500 years ago.

The Laika say that long ago, our planet was a poison-ous place for human beings, but Mother Earth buried these toxins in her belly so that the surface became a hospitable green and blue paradise. According to their ancient lore, the conquistadors would someday release these poisons, caus-ing the earth to become a toxic wasteland, and we humans wouldn't know how to contain these venoms. Nature itself would have to slowly recover her health.

Modern science validates this prediction. Two hun-dred and fifty million years ago, the earth's atmosphere primarily consisted of carbon dioxide (CO_2), which is very poisonous to humans. Then when green life appeared, the plants converted CO_2 into oxygen. This caused most of the airborne carbon to became trapped in the vegetation, which ended up in the subsoil and eventually became fos-sil fuels, buried in the deep strata of the earth. Now we're taking these fossil fuels from the great storage pits deep in the planet and burning them, releasing poisonous hydro-carbons into the atmosphere. We're headed toward creating the same environment that made it impossible for most creatures to exist on Earth, yet we're doing very little to reverse this dire situation. In fact, as global warming melts the polar ice caps, many individuals are eagerly preparing to drill for oil there, too.

Fortunately, there's a movement to bring back the old feminine ways and values. For instance, many people are rejecting the pyramidlike chain of command that's central to masculine theologies—the expectation that they must answer to priests, who answer to higher-level priests, who answer to popes, who answer to God. Many also refuse to subscribe to the belief propagated by scientists, which claims that anything that can't be measured, perceived, and controlled by using the five senses isn't real or true. They're no longer suspicious of their own hearts, and they don't feel that they must place their trust in dogma, or other people's interpretation of the sacred. They're beginning to look within and to nature for guidance.

An Experiential Knowledge

And the Lord God said, Behold, the man is become as one of us, to know good and evil: and now, lest he put forth his hand, and take also of the tree of life, and eat, and live forever: Therefore the Lord God sent him forth from the garden of Eden, to till the ground from whence he was taken.
— Genesis 3:22–23

In a feminine theology, the path toward enlightenment is an individual one. We're expected to trust in our own experiences, awareness, and interpretations. While the Laika value the path of prayer and meditation just as much as those who believe in a masculine theology do, they also recognize a third path to spirituality: that of direct knowledge. The Laika have no grand myth about the divine punishing humans for eating from the tree of knowledge of good and evil. Instead, they believe that we are meant to acquire wisdom, and that our error was in not eating enough of that fruit!

In the information age, we don't embrace knowledge that goes beyond mere facts and the logical arrangement of them. We have religions—along with countless practitioners of those faiths—but too often the spiritual essence of the teachings has been lost. We learn about interpretations of interpretations of the great truths, and we analyze and dissect those ideas, but we wouldn't think of going out into the desert for 40 days, as Jesus did, or sitting in meditation under the Bodhi tree, like Buddha. It's as if we're spending our time poring over hundreds of cookbooks filled with complex recipes and endlessly discussing the nutritional value of certain foods and diets, yet we never actually eat anything. Many people have lost the awareness of the value of directly experiencing the sacred . . . but, fortunately for us, following the practices of the four insights allows us to do just that.

The Four Insights

The wisdom of the Laika consists of four insights, each of which has four practices within it that allow us to move beyond mere understanding to actually experiencing shifts in perception—thus, helping us to transform ourselves and our world. The insights and their practices are:

- **Insight 1: The Way of the Hero**
  Practices: Nonjudgment, Nonsuffering, Nonattachment, Beauty

- **Insight 2: The Way of the Luminous Warrior**
  Practices: Fearlessness, Nondoing, Certainty, Nonengagement

- **Insight 3: The Way of the Seer**
  Practices: Beginner's Mind, Living Consequently, Transparency, Integrity

- **Insight 4: The Way of the Sage**
  Practices: Mastering Time, Owning Your Projections, No-mind, Indigenous Alchemy

I learned the four insights while under the tutelage of don Antonio. Together, we traveled from Lake Titicaca, the "sea on top of the world," through the Amazon, to the ruins of the desert kingdoms of Peru. He believed, as do I, that the new Earthkeepers will come from the land of the eagle—that is, from America and Europe. Now is the time for full disclosure of the insights. I believe that don Antonio trained me so I would become a bridge, bringing these wisdom teachings from the ancient Laika into the 21st century.

For the last 20 years, I have taught my students to use the insights for their personal healing and to assist others by working with the luminous blueprint of the body. Many of them have reported extraordinary results, healing themselves and transforming their lives and the lives of others. The insights have allowed them to become people of power and grace, and to walk the way of stewardship of the Earthkeepers.

If you want to begin living your life differently and perceiving your experiences through new eyes, it's important to go beyond mere understanding of the insights and actually follow their practices. This will allow you to change the core architecture of your luminous energy field. If you don't follow the practices, you may be inspired by the insights, but you won't be able to truly transform yourself. Mastering the energetic practices of the insights will free you from the confines of the story that has been written for you by your culture and your genes—the story of how you will live your life, react to the world around you, and die. You can become the storyteller of your own life, defying the old ideas about cause and effect and the limits of time.

In the following chapters, you'll learn about the four levels through which vibration and light creates all life: those of the serpent, jaguar, hummingbird, and eagle.

What's more, you'll learn practical tools that will help you dream a healthy, abundant, and joyous world into being—for yourself, for your loved ones, and for all people and creatures. You will become an Earthkeeper.

Part I

Understanding the Energy of Perception

The Four Levels
of Perception

In science, we believe that the universe works according to a set of precepts, or rules, which allow us to predict what will happen and respond appropriately to situations. Physics has its laws, mathematics has its theorems, and biology has its principles. For example, the tenets of math dictate that two plus two will always equal four, and the laws of physics assure us that objects will never fall upward.

Perhaps the most important rule in science is known as the law of cause and effect, or causality. That is, when an apple falls from a tree, we know it will hit the ground; when a pigeon poops above our car, we can be sure that it will land directly on our windshield; and when we accidentally forget an appointment to meet someone, we know that that person will be angry with us. We also feel secure in believing that if we apply ourselves and learn all the rules, as well as live by them, we'll have maximum control over our lives, and that will make us feel happy and safe.

When the rules are violated—when two plus two *doesn't* seem to add up in our lives—we feel angry and disoriented.

We can't quite comprehend the death of a healthy young person because we've been taught that if we live our lives the right way, we won't have to die for a very long time. Although we understand that we don't have complete control over events, we believe that as long as we do what we're supposed to do, we can count on nothing bad happening to us. Because we trust that causality is a reliable law of nature, we live by the rules and rarely attempt to break them.

For the Laika, however, synchronicity is the main operant law of life. They believe that while things may happen because of some earlier cause (for example, plant a seed and corn will grow), they just as often happen due to coincidence, serendipity, and circumstance. If two friends happen to bump into each other at a busy airport, then there is definitely a hidden reason why they were supposed to meet. The purpose for their meeting has yet to be revealed, though—it lies in their future.

How We Change Our World with Perception

All of us want to affect the world for the better. We look around us and see problems—crime, pollution, child abuse—and because we're a society of rules, we believe that laws and religious commandments will help us make changes. For example, Americans elect legislators to Congress who pass more and more laws every year in the hopes that these rules will make citizens' lives better.

By contrast, the ancient Greeks were a people of the *concept*—they knew that there was nothing as powerful as an idea whose time has come. Because they manipulated ideas so elegantly, they were able to invent democracy, develop philosophy, and systematize mathematics. Their Roman neighbors, on the other hand, were great lawmakers, and Roman codes have influenced many modern Western laws. When faced with problems, the Greek philosophers conceptualized new systems, while the Romans called on their armies to enforce the *precepts*.

The Laika don't live by rules or ideas. If they want to change their world, they don't pass new laws or come up with new theories. Instead, they choose to change the way they perceive a problem. By changing their *perception*, they transform a challenge into an opportunity. As you'll learn, the four insights and their practices will help you change your perceptions and allow you to dream your world into being.

Four Levels of Perception

Earthkeepers learn to experience events in such a way that they no longer take life personally, and they do so at the perceptual level of serpent. Here, things no longer happen to you; they simply happen. The pigeon doesn't poop on your car to make you upset; it simply poops, and your windshield gets smeared. It doesn't rain on you to make you wet; it simply rains.

When you change your perception of the events you experience, you also alter the way these situations live within you. You are no longer the cause or the effect of anything, and you sense a tremendous relief because the world is exactly as it should be—and it doesn't need you to fix it.

In the West, we tend to associate our perception with the dozens of states of awareness we're familiar with. For example, we're in one mode of awareness when we're just waking up or drifting off to sleep, another when we're in reverie, another when we're enraged, and so on. In each one, a different part of the brain is active—so we refer to them as "states of consciousness," which are products of the mind. Perceptual levels, on the other hand, exist independently of the mind. (In fact, the second level of jaguar, which we'll cover in a bit, contains the mind and all of its states of consciousness.)

There are four perceptual levels through which a Laika engages the world. These levels correspond to the four domains of manifestation of vibration and light: *the physical world* (our body), *the realm of thoughts and ideas* (mind), *the realm of myth* (soul), and the *world of spirit* (energy). These perceptual levels are associated with the four energetic bodies that make up the human energy field. They're stacked inside each other like Russian nesting dolls, with the physical body innermost, the mental body enveloping and informing the physical shell, the soul enveloping the mental and physical, and the spiritual body outermost, informing and organizing them all like a blueprint.

When we shift from one level of perception up to the next, we retain our ability to function at the lower realm, but we have a much wider view of what we're experiencing. I'm reminded here of an old story about a traveler who comes across two stonecutters. He asks the first, "What are you doing?" and receives the reply, "Squaring the stone." He then walks over to the second stonecutter and asks, "What are you doing?" and receives the reply, "I am building a cathedral." In other words, both men are performing the same task, but one of them is aware that he has the choice to be part of a greater dream.

Albert Einstein once said that the problems we face in life cannot be solved at which they were created. To that end, being able to shift to a higher realm of perception can help us find solutions to our problems, resolve conflicts, heal disease, and experience oneness with all of creation, whereas before we were only experiencing distress and separation.

In this chapter, you'll learn that there's a spiritual solution to every problem you encounter in the physical world, in your mind, and in your soul. You'll learn that you can't eliminate scarcity in your life by getting another job, or heal feelings of abandonment or anger by understanding your childhood wounds. *You can only fix these problems at the level above the one they were created in.*

The Laika associate each perceptual level with an animal that represents the powers and abilities one must acquire in order to influence reality in that realm. (Each level also has its own language that we can become fluent in.) Let's take a closer look at each of these levels now.

1. The Body and Physical Perception:
The Level of Serpent

The serpent is an instinctual creature with extraordinary senses that it can rely upon to tell it where there's food and where there's a predator. Similarly, in the physical realm, we humans rely on our senses to give us a picture of ourselves and the world. This is a very material level of perception, where everything is tangible, solid, and difficult to change; where reality is 1 percent spirit and 99 percent matter.

From the perception of serpent, we can see, touch, and even smell an object in front of us, such as a loaf of bread, and we know that it's there, physically present. We don't imagine the stalks of golden wheat in the bread, the kneading of the baker, or the fire that transformed it into a loaf we can eat—we only see an object that will satisfy our hunger. Similarly, we don't see sex as an act of love; we see it as a physical longing that will satisfy our desire.

At the level of serpent, the language we use to depict reality is molecular and chemical. We could describe bread scientifically, calling it "a food substance created from grain, yeast, and a few other ingredients; one that has a certain chemical makeup." We can also describe bread as a food, and we follow our instinct to eat it if we're hungry. Everything is as it seems: A loaf of bread is just that; a pigeon pooping is only that.

When we see problems through the eyes of the serpent only, we try to come up with physical solutions. We want to change the job, trade in the car, find a new partner, or have an affair. If we feel a headache coming on, we label it a "migraine" and reach for some medication. If we see a child acting out in class, jumping out of his seat to start wrestling with a schoolmate, we label him "naughty" and punish him. Sometimes these solutions work, but often they're too simplistic.

At serpent, we rely totally on our instinctual senses and don't reflect more deeply on our problems. We're operating from that part of the brain we share with lizards and dinosaurs—that is, we're aware of our physical bodies, but we're not cognizant of our mental, creative, and spiritual selves. In this state, we perceive outer form and accept only the obvious, remaining blind to our feelings and those of others. We're devoid of rich, complex thinking, and simply act and react. This state can be very useful for operating in the physical world. After all, we need to pay the bills, mow the lawn, and drive the kids to school without reading any more meaning into these actions. And, as Sigmund Freud once famously remarked, "Sometimes a cigar is just a cigar."

Remaining in serpent—that is, putting one foot in front of the other—is especially helpful for getting us through immediate crises. Our reptilian brain is in charge, working from survival instincts, and we simply do what has to be done without wasting valuable energy thinking about it, analyzing it, or getting emotionally distraught about it. We all know how wearying it is to meet someone who refuses to function at this level even when it's very practical to do so, choosing to read deep meaning into even the most trivial matters instead of just getting the work done.

The instincts of serpent are also very helpful because they can alert us to danger before we consciously perceive it—we get a "bad vibe" about a person or place and avoid it without knowing why, or we sense that a police officer with a radar gun is up the road, so we take our foot off the gas pedal.

Serpent is an essential state to master, as we have to be effective in the physical world and take care of business in a practical way. But when we allow our need to survive at all costs to dominate, we're not always so pleasant to be around. We reach for the most literal signs of security, such as having a big bank account and material toys; and we give into greed, stinginess, and suspicion. We coil up and contract, striking out before the other guy can clobber us; we amass weapons and build fences. In fact, archeologists excavating neolithic sites have found that the earliest defenses built by humans weren't designed to protect them from physical enemies but from the invisible ghouls and dangers they perceived from the state of serpent.

Unfortunately, much of humanity has lived at the level of serpent for thousands of years. Many people who take the Bible and the Koran literally, with their instructions to slay infidels, still live in this realm. It's important to be able to take our perception up a notch, for the good of ourselves and our world, because serpent is the cold-blooded domain of "an eye for an eye and a tooth for a tooth."

2. The Mind and Emotional Perception: The Level of Jaguar

In the next perceptual state, jaguar, the mind interprets our reality. We recognize that the mind can create psychosomatic disease or restore health, that repressed anger can cause cancer, and that a positive attitude brings joy and peace to ourselves and others around us. We're aware that our experiences are influenced by our thoughts and that everything isn't necessarily what it seems to be in the physical realm.

Now when we look at a loaf of bread, we know that it came from the fields of wheat and the baker, and we actually think about its many possibilities. We may choose to begin eating it, put it in the refrigerator and save it for later, or wrap it up and give it away to someone who is poor. We may add butter and garlic to it and bake it, or we may do something really unusual, such as tossing it across the room at someone and starting a food fight. But we've been taught certain beliefs about bread, and those beliefs influence our decision about what to do with it. We know that it's not right to waste food, so we quickly brush aside any temptation to throw it across the room just for fun.

In short, we understand that we have choices, but we also know that those choices are limited by our beliefs about bread. We also comprehend the bread's symbolic meanings:

We understand that it represents life, as in "the bread of life"; we use the expression "white bread" to denote a person who lacks dimension or personality; and we say, "I have no bread" to express a lack of money. A loaf of bread represents more than the satisfaction of our hunger, and having sex represents more than the satisfaction of our need—it can be an act of intimacy.

The realm of beliefs, ideas, and emotions is associated with the jaguar because this type of perception can suddenly transform situations, causing them to be seen in a new light, and such a creature is the archetype of sudden change. The jaguar spots his prey and pounces on it, quickly extinguishing its life—yet this helps keep down the population of the other animals and maintain balance in the rain forest, thus making it possible for other life to thrive in the ecosystem. In the same way, a single insight can allow us to break free from our negative feelings or an old way of operating that's preventing us from moving forward.

The jaguar's instincts are different from those of the serpent, which is solely concerned with survival and self-preservation. Jaguars are curious and inquisitive—our cat instinct leads us to the right people and situations (or the wrong ones, if our feline instinct is flawed). Jaguar perception is associated with the *mammalian brain,* that of emotion and deep feelings of love, intimacy, family, caring, and compassion. Yet it's also the brain of aggression, superstition, amulets, charms, and Nostradamus and Genghis Khan. The language of the level of jaguar is spoken or written words, which we use to form and express ideas, beliefs, and feelings. Here we understand symbols and signs and can agree that certain sounds are words that mean something specific.

From jaguar, we recognize that we can give a hungry man a fish, but a more practical long-term solution is to teach him how to fish. We know that we can give a starving child a piece of bread, but we also know that one does not live on bread alone. We rise above the literal level and see a wider range of possibilities in any situation. If we have a migraine, we ask ourselves, "What could be the cause? What is my body trying to tell me?"

Just as the mental level encases the physical, in jaguar we incorporate what we experience at serpent state. So if we have a headache, we're aware of our pain, but we also think about whether we could have consumed something that might have caused it, such as chocolate or red wine. We consider whether the migraine is a symptom of another type of ailment—maybe we're taking on more responsibilities than we can handle, or perhaps we're worried about our business or a fight with our spouse, and our body is responding by creating a headache.

Through the eyes of jaguar, we look at the child who is acting out in class and ask, "Is he actually unable to sit still and keep his hands to himself, and if so, why?" We consider whether the child ate a lot of sugary treats and has a strong physical urge to move, if he's bored by what the teacher is saying, and so on. We're able to perceive much more about the situation than we would at serpent state; consequently, we're able to think of many more solutions. We don't just punish the child who acts out, we make sure that he eats a healthy breakfast and has a chance to walk and run before he has to settle into his seat and focus on listening to the teacher. We don't just pop a pain pill—we learn to say no to our extra responsibilities and start expressing the anger we've been repressing. Because we have so many more possibilities, we're able to make effective changes and solve more complex issues.

3. The Soul and Sacred Perception: The Level of Hummingbird

The next domain of perception (which also encases the previous two levels) is that of the soul. The language of this level is image, music, poetry, and dreams—it's the realm of myth, where the soul can experience itself on a sacred journey, and is thus symbolized by hummingbird. Although tiny, this bird manages to navigate thousands of miles in its yearly migration from Canada to Brazil. It never loses its sense of direction or its drive to press forward, and never wonders if it has enough food or strength for its voyage. In the domain of the mythic, we are all like hummingbird, on a grand voyage and yearning to drink only from the nectar of life. When we don't perceive our journey as sacred, we become mired at the level of the mind and its complicated analysis of the world. From hummingbird, we perceive all of our experiences as part of an epic journey.

The hummingbird perceptual state is associated with the neocortex, the most recent addition to the human brain. The neocortex evolved around 100,000 years ago and is responsible for our ability to reason, visualize, and create. It is the brain of Galileo and Beethoven, science, art, and mythology.

At the soul level, solutions to problems that we can't solve with the mind suddenly become evident. In Peru a few years back, for instance, the native people had begun to perceive that the inexpensive, healthy, homemade, wholegrain bread that they'd been eating for generations was inferior to store-bought, heavily processed white loaves that they saw the wealthy eat. As a result, they were eating the less wholesome bread, and it was affecting the well-being of the population.

The president of Peru could have tried to resolve this problem at the level of the mind and attempted to convince people through a public-relations campaign that brown bread is good for you, or he could have worked with the legislature to pass a law raising the taxes on white bread to try to force people to buy more affordable loaves. Instead, he chose to address the situation from the hummingbird level of perception.

The president recognized that to the village people of his country, white bread had come to represent success and sophistication, while brown bread symbolized poverty and ordinariness. He knew he had to change their perception that white bread is better, so he made a television clip that showed him dining with his family in the presidential palace, eating brown bread. He knew that this would deliver the message that brown bread is the food of the successful and the sophisticated, and it worked. Indigenous people in Peru returned to eating brown bread because this was the bread of kings, not peasants!

When *I* eat at restaurants in Peru, I always load up my bag with the extra rolls that are served, because I know I'll have an opportunity to help someone out by giving them a roll that may be their only meal of the day. Once when I was traveling with a Laika elder, I found myself in a bus station surrounded by several children who had gathered around me in the hopes that I might give them some coins or candy. I began to take the rolls out of my bag and distribute them, but the elder told me, "This is not the bread these children need. The kind of food my people need is the food of the soul, not the stomach." He took the rolls from me and distributed them to the children himself, but as he did, he also began telling them stories about their Inka ancestors.

Afterward, the elder explained, "These stories are the nourishment that they are craving. I gave them not the bread that will feed them tonight, but the bread that will feed them throughout their entire lives." He was perceiving with the eyes of the hummingbird—to him, the stories were nourishment for the soul. When he saw me handing out rolls, he intervened at the level of the sacred by offering these children the mythology of their people.

At the level of the soul, things are what they truly are: an expression of the sacred. A house is not simply a roof over your head, it's a home. A spouse is not merely a person you share household and child-rearing duties with, but a chosen partner, a fellow traveler on a great journey. In this state, you look at bread and ask, "Am I hungry for bread, or am I hungering for the nurturing it represents?" You're able to understand the importance of breaking bread with others, and how your belly can never be adequately filled when others go hungry in the world.

At the level of hummingbird, we listen below the surface of conversations and hear their hidden messages. We operate in metaphors, so if we have a migraine, we ask ourselves, "Am I going out of my mind? What thoughts are stuck in my head? What is this a sign of?" In Chinese medicine, unexpressed anger is said to reside in our liver, so if we have liver trouble, we know it can be a sign of our repressed rage. So if our liver function is sluggish, we ask, "What medication can I take?" but also, "How can I practice forgiveness, both with myself and others?" We understand illness to be the warning light that tells us there's something going on that needs our attention, and we don't treat the symptom alone.

When we look through the eyes of hummingbird and see an overly active child, we ask, "How is this child's 'problem' a positive opportunity?" We recognize that giving Ritalin to a hyperactive child may make him stay in his seat and focus on what the teacher is saying to him, but it takes away his natural ability to multitask. In a jungle, this child's "problem" behavior or "learning deficit" would actually be an asset—he would be able to hear the birds call to each other and the rushing of the waterfall and still engage in a conversation, all the while remaining alert to possible danger. In hummingbird, we perceive the child's distractibility as a gift that's invaluable for his soul's journey.

At this level, we sense that we're all in a journey of growth and healing, making a trek back to where we were born to be, in a condition of divine well-being. If we experience a migraine, we ask ourselves, "What kind of healing is this headache calling me to?" It might be that we need to eat less chocolate, take medication, and stop putting ourselves through stress. It might also be that the way to cure our headaches involves a larger journey: Maybe we need to leave an unhappy relationship; perhaps it's time to move away from a remote rural area where we can't find work or create a sense of community; or we might need to let go of our disappointment in our parents and our anger at them, along with our fear that we're becoming just like them. We fix the headache by mending the soul. We see paths that will lead us back to health, and we undertake a healing journey.

Hummingbird is a much more commanding sphere for bringing about change than jaguar is. This is why visualization is so much more powerful than just reciting affirmations. When you want to ensure that your future holds a desirable outcome, you need to visualize it only once from the perceptual state of hummingbird. From jaguar, you would need to repeat the verbal affirmation dozens, or perhaps even hundreds, of times to achieve a similar result.

4. Spiritual Perception: The Level of Eagle

As the eagle soars above the valleys, he is able to visually take in the trees, the rocks, the river, and even the curvature of the earth . . . yet he's also able to spot a mouse 2,000 feet below him. His ability to see both the entire picture and a tiny piece of it at the same time are representative of the qualities of the level of Spirit.

In eagle, reality is 99 percent consciousness and 1 percent matter. There is little form or substance, and the language is energy. The brain associated with this level is the prefrontal cortex, which some neuroscientists call the "God-brain." In eagle, there is no longer a poor person receiving bread and a rich person handing it to him—there is only Spirit nourishing Spirit. We no longer perceive ourselves as disconnected from the planet or from other people; the boundaries melt away as our individual souls recognize our oneness.

I call this the "poof state" because at this level of perception, matter simply disappears. When we look at the hyperactive child, we see no illness or problems—there is simply God experiencing Itself as this child. When you ask a Laika who she is, she'll tell you, "The mountains am I, the river am I, the eagle am I, the rock am I." From jaguar, she may perceive herself as recovering from the loss of a loved one, but at eagle, she knows that she is God masquerading as herself, so she endeavors to take up permanent residence at the heights of eagle.

When we face a difficulty, the closer we can get to the level of Spirit, the less energy we need to effect change. Downstream, we can see war; but upstream, we can see the unrest among the people that will carry us to war, which is a much easier problem to address. Downstream is pollution; upstream is the question of why we're using plastic and throwing it on the ground. From hummingbird, we insist on recycling; from eagle, we question why we don't eliminate plastic packaging altogether. Downstream is our child having problems with the law or with relationships; upstream is the question of how we're teaching him by example to relate to and respect others.

At the lower levels of perception, we can try to figure out a way to prevent war or pollution, heal those who feel disenfranchised, or change those who insist on throwing away their garbage without recycling—but at the very highest level of eagle, we can actually become peace. We can become healing and beauty and embody the clean waters of a river. We stop perceiving a separation between us and our environment, or between us and other people.

One way to understand this highest level of perception, where our traditional ideas about the nature of reality dissolve, is to look at quantum mechanics. Physicists are discovering that at the subatomic level, matter is far less solid and tangible than we once thought it was. In other words, a solid table isn't solid at all, but a buzzing collection of particles and waves. Werner Heisenberg was the first to befuddle physicists with this notion, postulating in his "uncertainty principle" that when we observe an electron to measure its speed, this changes its position. So if we expect an electron to behave as a particle, it obliges; if we design an experiment where it must behave as a wave and strike two side-by-side targets simultaneously, it cooperates. This discovery was deeply disturbing to many scientists, including Einstein, who exclaimed that "God does not play dice" with the universe. And yet the Earthkeepers have always known that our perception of the world determines its very nature.

In other words, quantum physicists and Earthkeepers both suggest that the world is dreaming itself into being: The squirrels are dreaming it, the fish are dreaming it, and we are dreaming it—even the stones are dreaming it, although their slumber is deep and long. Quantum physics explains how it happens; the Laika tell us how to do it. Physics tells us how water evaporates into a cloud of vapor, while the Laika show us how to make it rain.

Of course, we humans experience reality through our own perception, not that of the elk or stone. Some Laika were said to be able to shape-shift and become a jaguar or eagle, able to sense the vegetation brushing against them as they slinked through the jungle or the wind rushing through their wings while soaring down into a valley. They did this to glimpse the world through the eyes of another, to discover whether there was a stream on the other side of the mountain or why the condors were becoming extinct.

In physics, chaos theory explains that a tropical storm in the Caribbean could actually be caused by a butterfly in Beijing that flapped its wings. It's very difficult to change a Category 5 hurricane (or late-stage cancer), but Earthkeepers know that from eagle, we can cross time and find that hurricane while it's still a whisper of wind on the edge of a butterfly's wing—that is, we can heal that storm before it's even born. This is the gift of this realm: There is no time, so we can change things before they come into existence. We can dream the world into being before energy ever acquires physical form.

◈

Using Different Levels of Perception

While we're always capable of interacting with all four levels of perception, we're usually bogged down in the physical body, or at best, caught up in the sphere of psychology and the mind. We believe that we could cure our unhappiness if only we could find a suitable relationship, or that the reason we can't stay on a diet is that we didn't receive the right nurturing from our parents. Occasionally, we're able to sense from hummingbird and hear the call to our epic journey . . . but then serpent drags us back, and we think that we don't have enough money or time, or we slip into jaguar and doubt whether we're strong or smart enough to walk the path.

At eagle, our power to affect reality is at its greatest. However, it takes courage and practice to shift into this high level of perception and stay there. The young Laika who are studying to become healers learn to diagnose and heal at the level of hummingbird. They don't work physically on the body or psychologically on the mind; instead, they learn to work with feathers, fire, and other tools that help them change the matrix of someone's luminous energy field. But the elders don't need to use a feather fan or herbs—they are working from eagle, where objects and thoughts and even visual images aren't necessary. They can heal without even moving a finger, as their presence alone will suffice.

In our own lives, we can use many tools to shift us into hummingbird perception, including meditation, prayer without words, music, and art. On a more superficial note, we can try dressing in vivid colors on a gray day to bring ourselves out of a depressive mood and into a brighter and more enthusiastic one; or we can recite prayers, hoping that speaking the words will shift us into truly feeling them. Yet at eagle, we won't need a bright yellow shirt to make us feel energized and excited about the day, even though it's been overcast and rainy for weeks. We won't need the words of the prayer because we can easily shift into the experience of sensing the divine in hummingbird and becoming one with Spirit in eagle. The shift happens within us.

Shifting to a Higher Level of Perception

When we get stuck in the perceptual landscape of serpent and jaguar, we spend a lot of time struggling with problems. If a man is having an emotional conflict with his wife, he will typically try to solve the crisis at the literal level by buying her something he thinks will make her smile again. When adolescents get depressed, they go to the mall or turn to drugs to heal their pain. Yet these quick fixes at the physical level never really work.

When you shift your perception to a higher level, you can transform the myriad challenges you're facing in your emotional and physical worlds. You can understand that what you perceive as a problem in one sphere is actually an opportunity at the level above it. The loss of a job or a relationship becomes an opportunity to reinvent yourself, while an illness offers you the chance to not just try to eliminate your symptoms but to also bring about deep healing and transformation. If you're sick, you can intervene at all four levels of perception: In serpent, you treat yourself with medicine; in jaguar, with psychology; in hummingbird, with meditation or spiritual practice; in eagle, with the awareness and wisdom of Spirit.

Shifting to a higher level of perception allows us to recognize that the reason we don't erect a dam that will make the darter snail extinct, or destroy the habitat of the spotted owl, is because they are representative of not just a few thousand animals, but of nature itself, which we must nurture and protect. We can then also begin to ask ourselves whether the hydroelectric power that a dam is going to produce to light up car dealerships at night is really even important. And at eagle, we can understand the hidden interconnectedness of things and perceive the synchronistic nature of reality—we recognize that there are no accidents and that everything has a purpose and a meaning. A loss isn't as devastating because we know there's a context for it, so when loved ones pass away, we know that they don't cease to exist, but are simply God seeking another expression and form.

All four perceptual states are helpful at different times. When you tumble down a ravine while hiking in an isolated area, you can go into serpent, let go of your fear, and access the resources of the reptilian brain to control the pain of your broken leg. Serpent (which is cold and indifferent and often associated with men in our culture) allows you to instinctively tend to your wound until you can crawl back to the trail and find help. In jaguar (which we often associate with women because it's intimate and emotional), you can process your feelings and experience your fear and vulnerability.

Moving to hummingbird, you begin to see the big picture: You become aware of the connection between your broken leg and your heavy burdens, and you recognize that in order to heal yourself, you have to be willing to let go of being in control all the time. And at the perspective of eagle, you can actually track along your future timeline and find a better outcome than dying alone in the woods, choosing a destiny in which help will find you. In eagle you can recognize that the healing you need may not be just the mending of your body but also of your soul, which longs to experience the lessons it came to learn on this earth, including why you injured yourself at that time and place.

I have seen many students leave the path of the Earth-keeper as soon as they start feeling better physically and emotionally, because they've met their needs at the levels of serpent and jaguar. Yet if they were perceiving from hummingbird, they'd recognize that feeling better is nice, but evolving to their highest capabilities is even more important. And if they were perceiving with the eyes of eagle, they would see that when they step into the fullness of their power, they can begin to dream their world into being, and that their own healing is directly tied to the healing of the entire planet. These students are like acorns beginning to sprout and pushing through the earth, and it's not much fun moving aside those mounds of dirt to get to the light.

During the course of my own training, there were times when I wanted to stop my work and just take it easy. I wanted to remain at the level of jaguar, where I was no longer bogged down by my problems or challenged or goaded to be the best I could be. But I recognized that in doing so, I'd miss the opportunity to grow my eagle wings.

Another advantage to being able to shift your perception is that if you're fated to develop a deadly disease because it runs in your family's genes, you don't have to engage it in the physical realm, where you'll actually develop the illness. At hummingbird, you can prevent sickness by learning the lessons that it came to teach you; while at eagle, you can clear the imprints in your luminous energy field that predispose you to this condition. If you have a book inside you that you've been struggling to write for ten years ("the great novel that will tell the story of my struggle," for example), you can bring it from the soul's domain into the literal realm and actually manifest that manuscript. Or if you're caught arguing with your romantic partner in the perceptual level of jaguar and both of you are stuck believing that you're right, you can get beyond blame. You can perceive the situation as an opportunity to connect with each other rather than as a chance to prove that you're correct and your partner is dead wrong.

While we may be drawn to one particular perceptual state (for example, we may engage the world primarily through jaguar and our emotions), we can learn to master all four levels with practice. Doing the following exercise will help you develop your ability to shift your perception. After you perform it a few times, you'll appreciate how the four levels are states that we gravitate to naturally, since they are the ways of "sensing" each of our four "sub-brains."

EXERCISE: Four Perceptions of the Face

This is a tracking exercise, in which you'll search for clues and information at each of the four levels of perception. (It can be done with a partner or alone.) Sit in a darkened room in front of a mirror, about four feet away from it, with a candle by your side. Practice deep, slow breathing as you gaze softly into your left eye, but do not stare. Count each inhalation until you reach ten, and then start again at one. Notice the play of light and shadow on your face, and keep focused on your left eye.

At the first level of serpent, notice how your face is as you've always seen it. Everything is exactly as it appears to be. This is the face you've looked at in the mirror a thousand times.

The second phase begins a few moments later—your face will begin to change as your perception adjusts from that of serpent to that of jaguar. You may see yourself shape-shift into an animal or take on the face of another person, or your face may disappear altogether except for your eyes. Don't be alarmed by what you perceive; instead, stay with your deep, regular breathing. Simply register the many faces that appear. . . . Some of them may be tens of thousands of years old; some may be the faces of former lifetimes; others are of power animals (your guides and allies in nature); and still other faces are those of your spirit guides. Track through this level and note all the faces you find.

When you reach hummingbird, your face will stop changing and you'll see just one image. Carefully observe the face that comes into stillness, for it has a meaning and a message that's important for you at this time. Hold it steady by focusing on your breath, and let it reveal its story to you. Who is it? Where did it come from? What messages does it have for you? The luminous energy field holds the memories of all of our former selves. Often these appear to be faces from a former lifetime, but they're frequently the faces of who we once were or might have become in *this* lifetime.

In the fourth stage, all images disappear, even your own face. When you reach eagle, all form dissolves into the universal energy matrix, leaving only Spirit and light.

To finish the tracking practice, take three deep breaths to bring yourself back to ordinary consciousness.

◈

I once performed this exercise with a client who had been diagnosed with a deadly medical condition. As we sat gazing softly into each other's faces, we only saw the other's eyes at first. Then as I entered jaguar perception, his face began to morph: He started to resemble an old man; then a young boy; and then an elderly Indian woman with long, flowing hair. These might have been the faces he wore in past lives or those of the stories that lived within him, yet I was looking for a particular one—the face of my client in the future after he was healed from his disease.

When I found it, I shifted my perceptual state to hummingbird so that the features would stop changing. This was the face we wanted for him: that of himself, healed. We had focused our intention on my finding that visage, and now that I had, I knew we had to install it into his destiny so that he would become the healed person represented by that face. Then I went into eagle and dissolved that expression so that I saw nothing but light. In my heart, I said, "May Thy will be done," so Spirit's will would prevail, not my own. (Note that it will require some practice for you to master the art of shifting into higher levels of perception, but don't worry—you can do it.)

I asked my client to continue this tracking practice on his own in front of the mirror, in order to draw his attention to his healed self and firmly install this face in his future. A few months later, he went into full remission from his condition.

In the following chapter, you will learn more about your own energetic anatomy, including the luminous energy field and the chakras, and how they relate to the four levels of perception and the four insights.

Your Energetic
Anatomy

Most of us know a little about how our physical bodies work, and we may even be aware of how our thoughts and emotions can affect us, and vice versa. Yet in order to gain access to the higher levels of perception that will allow us to dream our world differently, we need to learn more about the anatomy of the soul and the spirit. We need to understand how our emotions, our beliefs, and the colored lenses through which we perceive reality are held in the luminous energy field (LEF), the aura of energy and light that surrounds each one of us.

The LEF is the blueprint for our lives, containing the chronicles of our pain and suffering and the pathways to our healing. In fact, we are able to teach our students at the Healing the Light Body School how to read the stories etched in a client's LEF, as well as how to decipher the emotional and physical conditions that afflict him or her.

Imagine that you're surrounded by a bubble of light that extends about the width of your outstretched arms and down into the earth about a foot. Streams of energy continually circulate through your LEF, since it contains the acupuncture meridians and the chakras (which I'll explain in just a bit). Running through the middle of this pulsating orb is a very narrow, tubelike hole, less than a molecule wide, making the luminous energy field like a big oval bead (or, as it's called in geometry, a *torus*).

When we die, the LEF passes through this narrow tunnel back to the spirit world, like a doughnut going through its own hole—this is the dark passageway that people who have had near-death experiences report traveling through as they journey back home. We can learn to access the higher levels of perception by working with our LEF and its structures: the chakras and the assemblage point.

The Nine Chakras

We all have nine chakras, or energy centers, in our bodies, lined up along our spine. While Eastern traditions recognize seven chakras, the Laika recognize an eighth one, which is like a radiant sun located above the head, outside the physical body but within the LEF. (In the West, we call this eighth chakra the "soul.") The ninth chakra is high above it, existing outside of time in the center of the cosmos, and connecting us with all of life. The ninth chakra is Spirit.

Each chakra is a vortex of swirling light extending a few inches outside of our body and spinning in a clockwise direction, and the point of the vortex connects to our spine and to our endocrine glands. Our chakras inform our neurophysiology directly by downloading information from the LEF into the central nervous system. Because they also connect to our glands, they affect the levels of all our hormones, influencing our moods, our weight, our blood chemistry, and our immune system.

The chakras are gateways through which your brain and nervous system can interact with the four levels of manifest creation. Through the first chakra, you engage with the level of serpent—the dense physical and biological energies. The second chakra allows you to engage the level of jaguar—emotions such as anger and fear, as well as the more refined feelings of love and compassion. The sixth chakra allows you to engage the level of hummingbird—the divine energies found in sacred places or accessed through meditation, prayer, and mystical experiences. The ninth chakra allows you to engage the level of eagle—the indefinable source of all creation, where you can dream the world into being.

Let's take a brief look at each energy center now.

— The **first chakra** is at the base of the spine, near the tailbone, and it connects us to Mother Earth. It's where our primitive instincts are energetically located, and it's associated with the perceptual state of serpent. (In many Eastern traditions, the serpent energy of the *kundalini* is also said to reside in this chakra.) When we clear our first energy center, we let go of the fear of scarcity and become more open to the abundance that surrounds us.

— The **second chakra** is located four fingers below the navel, and it's the seat of our passions. This is where all of our feelings and emotions live energetically, and our self-esteem and sense of how we are loved or unloved also reside here. Our anger clogs this chakra, as does our fear of being physically or emotionally in danger. When we clear it, we open ourselves up to creativity and romantic intimacy. This chakra is associated with the perceptual state of jaguar, and it's connected to our adrenal glands and the fight-or-flight response.

— The **third chakra** is at the solar plexus and is associated with the body's physical energy level. Clearing it allows us to be successful in the world, have good relationships with others, and be clear about who we are and how we want to express ourselves.

— The **fourth chakra** is at the center of the chest, and it's associated with the heart. It is where we experience love for all people and creatures, for rocks and waterfalls, and for deserts and oceans. The heart chakra is the central point in our physical energy system, as there are three chakras above it and three below. When we clear this area, we rid ourselves of egotism and open ourselves up to our greatest capacity for intimacy.

— The **fifth chakra** extends from the hollow of the throat, and it's our psychic center. When this area is clogged, we fixate on our own group or tribe and our own opinions. When we cleanse it, however, we recognize our connection to others, become better communicators, and are open to gaining knowledge by listening to people even when we may not agree with them.

— The **sixth chakra** (or "third eye") is located in the middle of the forehead. It's where we experience our relationship to everything and everyone, along with our awareness that we are eternal beings. This is the center where the divine resides within us, and it's associated with the perceptual state of hummingbird. When this chakra is clogged, we can become spiritually arrogant, knowing facts about the sacred but not practicing them.

— Located at the very top of the head, the **seventh chakra** is our doorway to heaven, connecting us to the stars. Clearing this energy center allows us to experience time as nonlinear and break free of the laws of cause and effect. When the seventh chakra is clogged, we mistakenly believe that we've achieved enlightenment, not realizing that we have farther to go before reaching that egoless state.

— The **eighth chakra,** which is a few inches above our heads, is where we experience a union with all of creation and its Creator. When this energy center is clogged, we can find ourselves caught between Spirit and matter, living only partially in our bodies, and feeling dissociated and disconnected from all. This chakra corresponds to the soul—etched in its walls are the imprints of trauma that we bring with us from one lifetime to another and that helped select the parents we were born through. These imprints predispose us to living, learning, aging, and dying in particular ways, and are mirrored by the imprints in our LEF.

— Finally, the **ninth chakra,** which exists outside of time and space and is always crystalline and pure, is where we can experience the magnificent expanse of creation. This is where we reside within God. To reach this area, we ascend the silver cord of light that rises up from the eighth chakra—it resides at the heart of the universe, and is Spirit. There is only one ninth chakra, for there is only one of us in Spirit. This chakra is associated with the perceptual state of eagle.

To follow the practices of the four insights, it's important to first clear the negative energy, or "psychic sludge," that clouds our chakras so that we no longer project our wounded selves into the world and confuse that for reality. This is important for all the chakras, but especially the first, where the perception of serpent is located; the second, where jaguar lives; and the sixth, the mythical third eye, where hummingbird resides. Cleansing your energy centers will allow them to carry new information into your body and nervous system. And as you clear the first seven, the eighth will gradually cleanse itself, erasing the imprints of karma, trauma, and disease that propel you unconsciously from one lifetime to the next. (The ninth chakra can never become clogged, because it is Spirit itself.)

Clearing the chakras is like wiping clean the lenses of perception that allow you to see and interact with the four levels of creation. When your chakras are clogged, you remain trapped in the physical and mental, the most crude realm of experience. In the following exercise, you will learn to cleanse the psychic debris that has settled in each of your energy centers.

EXERCISE: Clearing the Chakras

Begin by finding a quiet spot. (I suggest doing this exercise while lying comfortably in your bed.) Close your eyes and take a few deep, focused breaths. Let your thoughts float in front of you, paying no attention to them, as you continue to inhale and exhale.

Bring your hands together in the prayer position in front of your chest, with your fingertips touching. Rest your hands against your chest as you maintain this pose. Inhale deeply . . . and exhale. Inhale . . . and exhale. Breathe deeply several times.

Separate your hands, shake them vigorously, and then return them to the prayer pose. Notice the feeling of energy coursing between your fingertips—then separate your hands very slowly, maintaining this feeling. With your eyes closed, try to see if you can perceive the threads of light between your fingertips, creating a sensation of tingling or warmth.

Move your right hand over your first chakra, to its wide mouth two inches away from your skin. Feel its energy as it spins clockwise. (Some say this feels like cotton candy, while others experience it as a light, tingling sensation.) Now begin "unwinding" the chakra by slowly spinning your hand counterclockwise ten times, imagining your body as the face of the clock and your fingers as the hands. Explore the inside of this funnel of light with your fingertips, sensing its energy and noting whether it is cool or warm, tingly or sludgy. Feel the stream of toxic energy flowing out of your chakra and into the earth as you "backwash" this chakra. Now return your first energy center to its normal direction of spin by slowly turning your hand clockwise ten times.

Because every chakra is associated with particular feelings, as you cleanse each one you may notice that certain emotions or memories arise spontaneously. Allow these sensations to wash through you *without analyzing them.* You're doing this work at the level of eagle, of energy, so don't distract yourself with psychological stories or explanations for these feelings. For example, the second chakra governs the fight-or-flight response, and when you clear it, you might remember the last time you felt frightened or in danger, or you might reexperience the feelings themselves. If this occurs, allow the sensations to pass through you like a soft breeze. They will subside on their own after you've taken a few deep, slow breaths. (Please note that you may not feel any sensations as you do this practice. If this is the case, don't worry—the exercise is effective and powerful, whether you experience any feelings or not.)

Repeat this unwinding action with each of the seven chakras to cleanse them of any psychic debris, and then be sure to rewind them. Now imagine that you are hovering a few inches above your physical body. After a few minutes, cross your hands over your chest and take three deep breaths. Fully inhabit your body again. Shake your hands vigorously and knead them together. Rub your face with your hands and open your eyes.

— *Intermediate level:* After you've done this exercise a few times and can sense your luminous self floating above your physical body, direct your awareness into your eighth chakra. Allow your consciousness to inhabit this space where the divine resides within you. Explore the vastness of this domain, and try to remember what you were before you were born and what you will be after you die. Remember that this chakra exists outside of time, and here you can recall events that occurred in the past and the future.

— *Advanced:* After you master the above technique, perform the exercise again; only this time direct your awareness into your ninth chakra. Experience yourself dissolving and becoming one with Spirit and with the vast expanse of creation.

We call this center a chakra for lack of a better name. In reality, it's the dwelling place of Spirit, which is everywhere, in the manifest and unmanifest creation.

The Assemblage Point

The assemblage point is an energetic structure within the LEF where we decode all our supersensory experiences, from déjà vu to precognition, to bliss and love, to having a sense of foreboding about something or someone, and to knowing that the telephone is going to ring before it actually does. It's the luminous equivalent of our physical brain (and about the same size, but shaped like an orb), and it is here that we take in the information our ordinary senses can't grasp. So while our hand can detect the touch of our beloved but can't feel the love conveyed by that touch, the assemblage point *can* interpret the meaning of this contact, and it builds an internal picture of our psychological and spiritual reality.

To understand how our assemblage point works, we can compare it to how we process visual information. The eyes receive photons of light reflecting off the ocean and the sand. These electrical impulses travel through the optic nerve to the visual cortex in the brain, which creates an image inside our heads. We call this image "the beach" and project it onto the outside landscape, but all seeing really happens inside the brain.

In a similar manner, our assemblage point decodes information received through our chakras and "reads" the world of energy and emotions around us. We call this image "reality" and project it onto our surroundings and the people we come in contact with. But the Laika understand that all reality only actually exists inside ourselves.

The assemblage point is located within the LEF (its exact location differs for everyone)—just as there are centers in the brain that process information from our senses, this grapefruit-sized torus processes psychic and emotional information. In our assemblage point, we have filters for our reality that are based in our culture, gender, age, and so on. In the West, for instance, we see the color red and think *Danger!* or *Warning!* or *Excitement and rebelliousness,* and we become more alert. However, in the East, red is perceived as a color of good fortune that brings joy and contentment.

Our assemblage point is attuned to interpret certain valences and frequencies, which are determined mostly by our life experiences. If we don't have those valences programmed into our assemblage point, we won't perceive them. For example, if we dwell in a city and travel to the jungle, even though our ears have the same structural mechanisms of the rain-forest native, we simply wouldn't have the sensitivity to hear certain birds that alert us to the presence of snakes that the native does. Those of us who live in cities become so accustomed to hearing loud sounds within ten feet of us that we're not used to perceiving sounds from far away—it's almost as if we're auditorily nearsighted. Neuroscientists believe that these pattern-recognition abilities are wired into pathways inside the brain. But the brain is simply the hardware for the Laika; the software that drives it is programmed into the assemblage point inside the luminous energy field.

If we lived in perfect communion with nature, our assemblage point would sit on the eighth chakra six to eight inches above our heads, in a position I call "bridge." When our assemblage point is in bridge, all of our instincts are recalibrated to their original settings. From bridge, we can move our assemblage point to the second chakra to perceive with the senses of jaguar and actually reset the instincts of that chakra—for example, we'll no longer get involved with the wrong people just because we're attracted to those who are similarly wounded. We can move our assemblage point to sense from the level of serpent when it is practical to do so, but we won't get stuck there, unable to think more deeply about our choices. Whatever level we are engaged with, our vision and our instinct won't be clouded.

Because we don't live in nature, and we also need to be functional in a very dysfunctional world, our assemblage point ends up being skewed to one direction. In the West, the assemblage point tends to be located to one side of the head because we're very rational, thought-driven people. We're attracted to others who have an assemblage point that is similar in valence and position because we feel in sync with them. We typically perceive someone with a very different assemblage point as strange or foolish, and we may even think that they're stupid because they can't perceive what we can, or loony because they sense what we don't. We don't realize that our perceptions are limited by our beliefs and life experience. Just like the blind Indian men who examined an elephant in the ancient story, one of us feels the elephant's tail and pronounces that the crea-ture is like a rope, another feels the tusk and insists that it's like a sword, while another wraps his arms around the beast's leg and swears that the elephant is like a tree. For each man, the limited reality he perceives seems to be the only reality.

Your assemblage point typically remains in the same location throughout your life—a place I call the "access" position—because this is where you access your ordinary reality. But you can learn to move it and alter your perceptions, and therefore change your experience of reality. In the exercise that follows, you'll learn to locate your assemblage point and move it, first to bridge, and then to each of the four chakras associated with the four levels of perception.

Once you move your assemblage point to the bridge position, you can cross over to any of the four perceptual levels. In fact, you can *only* change levels by going through bridge (which is why we call it so). It's helpful to imagine bridge as the center of a wheel, and the four perceptual levels as the four cardinal directions of north, south, east, and west—or you might think of it as "neutral" in a car, which you shift to between gears.

At the end of the exercise, you'll return the assemblage point to access, its original location. If you left the assemblage point at bridge, you would experience a blissful state, but you couldn't very well respond to the dog that's barking to go outside, or the ringing telephone. While it's excellent to meditate in bridge position or stay there for a while and reside within your own soul space, it's an impractical state to be in for long . . . unless, of course, you're in a monastery and don't have to walk the dog or communicate with the world.

The purpose of this exercise is to learn how to shift perceptual levels more readily. It will require practice—but as you master it, you'll be able to change the energetics of any situation you find yourself in and solve problems from a higher level. The paradox is that you can only change the world when you realize it's perfect exactly as it is *for that level*. This is the understanding you achieve when you perceive a problem from the level above the one at which it was created. From this level, you will sense only possibilities and have the freedom to change anything.

EXERCISE: **Moving Your Assemblage Point**

Find a quiet and comfortable spot in which to sit where you won't be interrupted. Turn off all phone ringers, settle into your chair, or find a comfortable position on the couch. Let go of the thoughts that are tumbling around in your mind. Inhale deeply, and exhale. Breathe in . . . and exhale. Slowly inhale again, focusing on your breath . . . and exhale again.

Place both of your hands in a prayer pose at the center of your chest. Take a few breaths slowly and then raise your hands, still pressed together, up past your face, above your head, pushing them upward as high as you can until you enter the eighth chakra, a golden disk of energy that hovers, spinning, several inches above your head and within your LEF. This chakra is the soul, and it exists outside of time and is eternal.

Pull your hands apart and fan them outward, palms facing away from each other, like a peacock spreading its fan. Set your intention to expand your eighth chakra to envelop your entire body. As you do so, you're expanding your LEF from its contracted, cocoonlike state, stretching your light into a bubble that surrounds you.

Continue to breathe slowly as you bring your hands back to prayer position at your chest . . . then reach outward to expand your luminous energy field to your sides.

Repeat this motion at the level of your belly, your chest, and your pelvis, expanding your LEF by using your imagination and your hands. Be aware of this bubble of light that surrounds you, pulsating as it draws energy up from the ground and into your legs, spine, chest, arms, and head. Feel the energy as it flows from above your head back to the ground, and comes back up again through your feet.

Using your hands, explore the inside of your LEF until you sense a spot that feels different—it may be tingly, warmer, or cooler than the rest of your energy field. Remember that your assemblage point will most likely be located near your head, to one side or the other, and it will feel like a ball about the size of a grapefruit. When you find it, bring your other hand upward and feel its spherical shape (use your imagination). What sensations do you experience as you hold your assemblage point? As my students sometimes report, you may encounter an unexpected feeling of joy, or even nausea or disorientation. This is not uncommon, as you're about to change the way that you perceive your world. (Other students have reported feeling nothing, and they simply imagine what it would be like to hold this energy sphere in their hands. If this also applies to you, that's absolutely fine.)

Now move your assemblage point by bringing your hands to your eighth chakra, right above your head, to the bridge position. Take a few deep breaths, holding your assemblage point in its natural state, and note the sensations in your body; for example, it's not unusual to experience feelings of peace and communion while in this position. I tell my students who have a difficult time when they try to meditate to attempt to do so after they've moved their assemblage point to bridge, where contemplation and meditation come naturally. In this position, the mind quiets, and an hour can go by in what seems like just five minutes.

The 8th Chakra

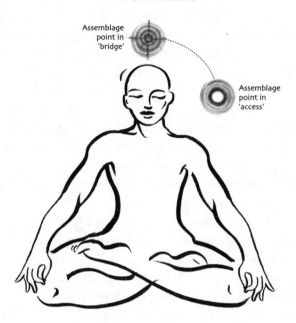

Assemblage point in 'bridge'

Assemblage point in 'access'

Continue to breathe slowly and deeply, and release your assemblage point. Notice if it remains at your eighth chakra or if it hovers back to its usual position in access. (Keep in mind that it will take several attempts before you master holding your assemblage point in bridge.) Next, bring your assemblage point down to your first chakra, the domain of serpent, which is located at the base of your spine, near your pubic bone. This vortex of energy opens outward, stretching a few inches outside your body. Hold your assemblage point here. Because serpent is located at your first chakra, it is a very primordial, instinctual state—

become aware of how your breathing changes, and how easily you can tune in to your heart rate, to the sensations in your skin, and to your physiology.

When you're ready, raise your assemblage point back up to the bridge position. Rest there briefly. Inhale deeply and slowly, and then exhale. Now bring your assemblage point to your second chakra, the vortex of energy located below your navel. Rest it there, experiencing the sensory level of jaguar. Because the perception of the cat is located at your second chakra, it can arouse emotions and even sexual feelings. Become aware of which emotions reside here, and how easily you can sense anger, excitement, or fear; as well as kindness, generosity, and passion. Continue breathing deeply and slowly, and return your assemblage point to the position of bridge.

Slowly move your assemblage point to the sixth chakra, in the middle of your forehead, the realm of hummingbird. Rest in this level of perception, aware of the many paths that your journey has taken you on in this life. Here you can observe how everything that's happened to you, good and bad, has had meaning and purpose. Because the sixth chakra is the domain of inner vision, you may feel a sense of stillness, similar to how a hummingbird hovers in flight. In this perceptual state, telepathic experiences are common, and an Earthkeeper can sense what a loved one is doing or how she is feeling, even at a distance of hundreds of miles.

When you're ready, return your assemblage point to bridge. Take a few deep breaths . . . now move your assemblage point up to the ninth chakra, located high above your head and outside of your LEF, the domain of Spirit and eagle. Experience a blissful connection to all that is: to the rivers and the trees, to the people living now and to your ancestors, to the rain and the wind, to the stars and the sun. Experience your oneness with the divine and all of creation, beyond boundaries of space and time.

When you're ready, pull your assemblage point back to bridge. Take a deep breath, and move your assemblage point back to access. Here, you reenter your everyday reality and return to being fully functional in this world. Finish by bringing your hands back to prayer pose for three deep breaths.

◇

When you master the art of moving your assemblage point, you can intervene at other levels of reality to heal yourself or even to regain the extraordinary creativity you had when you were young. I once worked with children in a Head Start program, and at the beginning of the year, before they'd become accustomed to the rules of preschool, I asked them to sketch a house. Their drawings were of the most fantastic structures—houses floating on clouds, entwined in the roots of a tree, or sailing on rivers. By the end of the year, these boys and girls had learned the rules of ordinary perception, and they believed that a "proper" house consisted of a big square with little square windows and an angular roof, which was topped with a little rectangular chimney that had a curl of smoke coming from it. Even the kids who lived in crowded housing projects drew houses like this because they had learned the perceptual filters of the culture. Unconsciously, they were entering the same cultural trance we've all been educated into. They had become citizens of the dull, flat land of ordinary reality.

When our assemblage point locks into place and tunes out the other frequencies of reality, we call it "maturity."

In other words, we no longer see fairies frolicking near the creek or perceive monsters under the bed—instead, we see problems and not opportunities. This is why someone who works in advertising, an industry that demands a high level of creativity, will fill her office or cubicle with wind-up toys and foam-rubber basketballs and hoops, using such playthings to help her get back in touch with the creative child she was instead of the logical, sensible adult she has become.

Moving the assemblage point to each of the four perceptual states allows us to break out of the flatland perspective on reality and tap in to an infinite range of possibilities. And when we enter the state of eagle, we can resolve problems at their source and gaze with the eyes that have seen the birth and death of galaxies.

I had the opportunity to experience this in my own life. My Laika mentor, don Antonio, used to tell me that I was an interior decorator of my psyche. Once while we were traveling to an oxbow lake that was fed by the Amazon River, he explained that I was like that lagoon—I perceived myself to be separate from the great river of life, and I would gather driftwood and flotsam to build dream castles on the shores of my lagoon. He was trying to teach me that I was caught at the level of serpent, attempting to change the world at the most dense and material level, and that this absorbed 95 percent of my energy. When my castles collapsed, I'd haul the driftwood to the other end of the beach and start building them all over again, creating a new relationship, a new project, or even a new career, all of which took many months of effort.

Don Antonio would tell me, "I could put my hand at the source of that river and create a ripple that will change the contours of your shoreline downstream. Or if you've fallen out of your canoe, that current might wash you ashore and save your life. I could create this powerful wave with just the tiniest amount of my energy."

Working at the literal level to construct what I thought would be a happy and fulfilling life required enormous amounts of strength and attention. My mentor was trying to tell me that I needed to travel further upstream and, from the perceptual state of eagle, affect the flow of the river that fed my lagoon and caused it to overflow and destroy my castles. The only way to do this was to raise my level of perception.

In addition to learning the perceptual states, I had to master the practices of each insight. Only then did I stop trying to fashion a life with just the right job, personal relationships, and projects, as if there were a simple mathematical equation for happiness. Instead, I learned to operate from a higher perspective and open up to wider definitions of joy and success. Then I discovered the power to create a different story for myself and the world. Only then could I create a new and better dream. Only then could I let go of the stories I kept retelling myself . . . which were trapping me in a limited existence.

It is now time to move on to Part II of the book and get to know each of the four insights intimately. In the next chapter, I will explain how we walk through our lives unconscious of the fact that we're following old, deadening scripts, and how we can shed our serpent skin and be reborn into a more creative way of living.

The Four

Insights

of strength, its dignity and beauty, you represent
the manifestations of the Love, Kindness, etc.

INSIGHT 1

The Way of the Hero

To be a hero means being the author of your own myth.

The first insight is the way of the hero because when you follow its four practices, you turn your wounds into a source of power. While you have certainly been emotionally hurt in some way (as we all have), when you walk the way of the hero, the traumas you have experienced can actually help you find your strength and compassion.

You can accomplish this by shedding the stories of your past, just as a snake sheds her skin. In the process, you will cease being a victim of what happened to you and instead become empowered to write your own valiant tale of strength, healing, and beauty. You no longer have to be the misunderstood artist, the tough rebel with the heart of gold, the innocent who's been betrayed, or the child of the abusive parent.

The first insight shows you that these are merely characters you've created to explain what happened to you. Your personal stories are just yarns you've spun; they are not *you*. Suffering occurs when you believe them to be true—whether you created these stories yourself or someone else did it for you, you confuse them for reality. The characters in your narrative then become like hungry ghosts who show up at the dinner table and feed off your scraps.

You may strive to understand and negotiate with these ghosts because you believe that they're genuine. But their complaints, demands, and thirst for attention are endless: The shadow of your father hovers over you, seeking forgiveness or retribution; the image of your children tells you that you should have raised them differently; and the specter of your youth haunts you, berating you for having squandered it. You are bombarded by the shrill voices of all those you've wronged or been wronged by . . . and they never shut up.

In fact, if we feed these hungry ghosts, they will suck the life force right out of us. (After all, how many people in their 50s do you know who are still struggling with the memory of a neurotic mother or distant father?) We can pat ourselves on the back for surviving a difficult childhood or we can rationalize our behavior patterns by pointing to the racism or gender discrimination we suffered, the way our parents neglected us, or to any number of logical reasons for why we act the way we do. As long as we cling to the belief that these stories are real, we stay stuck, continually feeding the hungry ghosts in a dreary process that mimics, yet forestalls, true healing.

Too often we work overtime to meet the requirements of our story. How many family rituals continue because everyone is convinced that they have to perform them in order to express their love and loyalty to their parents, children, and siblings? How many people spend their lives in meetings that have little practical purpose except to perpetuate the idea that productive individuals attend lots of important meetings? How many students force themselves to choose practical courses of study rather than following their heart's interest? When you banish the ghosts from your table and let go of your stories about what is "proper," "appropriate," and "best," you free yourself to explore the mystery of who you and the other people in your life truly are.

The first insight is associated with serpent—the physical body, the material world, and sensory perception—and as you master it, you'll start to see beyond the most simplistic, literal level of reality. You'll begin to recognize the events from your early life that shaped and molded you, as well as how your parents and culture affected who you've become. And then when you outlive *that* story, you can craft a new one that's better suited to a hero's journey. You can let go of the tedious tale of a middle-aged man reliving his adolescence, or a woman in her 40s trying to look and act as if she were in her 20s, and write a far more original story for yourself. You will recognize the divine choreography of events in your past that have propelled you on your journey of healing, learning, and discovery.

The Physical Manifestations of Our Stories

Our stories are so powerful and convincing that they get internalized and become lodged in our muscle tissue as cellular memories. So when we "somatize" these tales, the way we walk and talk changes. We might forget that we're poets and not just parents, and find ourselves speaking in baby talk. We may convince ourselves that we're perpetual victims and, instead of striding confidently, shuffle along with eyes cast downward and shoulders hunched. Actors who want to truly inhabit a role will often start by carefully observing the physical characteristics and movements of an angry young man, a depressed middle-aged woman, or a wide-eyed innocent—they understand that these people's stories manifest in their physical appearance and movement.

Whatever your image of who you are in your story, you will embody it, and people will respond to you as such. The way you look and act will send the message that you're unapproachable or friendly, confident or insecure, powerful or wounded. Also, whether you realize it or not, you'll beam at others who are supposed to be in your circle and shun those whose body language or looks signal that they don't belong in your world (because you're buying into *their* stories). Think about the people you sit down next to on a crowded bus—they're probably the ones who are most likely to be in your social circle rather than those who look, dress, and act unlike you.

I'm reminded of when I spent a summer in a seedy part of New York City several years ago. The first few days, I observed that the street was full of muggers and rapists, yet over the ensuing weeks, I discovered that these "sinister characters" were just my neighbors. And they were the nicest people—they had simply adopted a look that ensures that you command respect in New York City. Soon after this realization, I saw a menacing character reflected in a shop window and became frightened. That's when I understood that I, too, had developed an attitude and a look that demanded respect in the streets, and I barely recognized my own self.

Why We Cling to Our Stories

We cling to our tales because we derive some benefit from them, even when they also cause us suffering. Usually, the main payoff is that our ego is able to be a star if we remain part of the drama. We believe that someday we'll overcome our terrible childhood or disaster-prone love life if we work hard enough at fixing ourselves, but we don't consider letting go of the role of victim. Doing so would require us to release the ego's need to be in charge of telling the story.

Your ego has a very strong survival instinct and will do just about anything to stay alive. It will fight the longing to heal, and insist on its need to be right. You may have experienced this when you were arguing with someone: There was a part of you that wanted to stop jousting and instead find common ground with him or her, but your ego insisted that you knew more or had the superior point of view, so it demanded that you keep fighting until the other person was vanquished. Your ego has convinced you that if you let go of your story, you won't be loved, valued, recognized, or seen—you might even disappear.

Often, the benefit of clinging to our stories is that they give us a false sense of security and purpose. After all, who are we if we're not the wise authority figure, the creative rebel, or the nurturing parent? In my early days, when I practiced psychology, I would hear people talk about their life stories, claiming their right to feel victimized by their childhoods, spouses, or finances. Inevitably, they got sick of these unoriginal yarns that only served to trap them in their suffering. Yet they knew no other way—they found themselves repeating the same drama over and over again, with different jobs, partners, and friends. Sometimes they would even leave therapy when I explained that they weren't the only ones bored to exhaustion with their tales. (In those days, I was young and didn't know how to assist my clients in forging a new story, a heroic myth that would be empowering instead of deadening.)

In actuality, our story becomes a death sentence for the hero within, because it demands denying what doesn't fit into its narrowly defined roles. I have children, for instance, but I'm not "a father." Of course I do fathering, and I believe that I do it well, but that doesn't define who I am. I also do writing and healing, but I'm not a writer or a healer. Who I am is a mystery that I uncover more clues to every day. Some days I feel completely befuddled about who I am, but I don't let that get in the way of my doing good, effective parenting. It's just that I recognize that a character like "father," "writer," or "healer" is far too small to describe what I am.

If you identify yourself as a parent, remember that your children will outgrow their need for a mother or father who takes care of them. Who will you be when your children leave home? How will your role shift? Many parents become depressed when their last child moves away, as the empty-nest syndrome forces them to face the fact that they are no longer needed to wash their child's clothes or make sure he eats three square meals a day. Similarly, if you identify yourself as an entrepreneur, a writer, a healer, a husband, or a wife, you'll come to the end of that role someday. You'll have to create a new identity for yourself at that point, and it can be frightening because you don't know if you will find an identity that has meaning for you.

Every character in your story presents false evidence of your true nature. And when you insist on only seeing others—whether it's your mother, your father, your boss, or your child—in the role they play in your life story, your perception will keep you from experiencing who they really are. This will create anger in you and in them. However, when you let go of your story, your relationships with those you love and struggle with will begin to heal, and the resentments will dissolve.

Dropping Our Roles

Every story has a cast of leading characters who play certain roles. When we practice the way of the hero, we drop the limiting characters we identify with, along with the beliefs that these characters hold to be true. Our characters become what we *do,* but they are not what we *are.* We can continue to perform as a nurse, mother, son, salesperson, real estate agent, or retiree, and can be immensely effective at each of these tasks. We can be in the world but not possessed by that which is ultimately unimportant. In other words, we are not the laundry, the cooking, or the cleaning—we simply do these things without pain or struggle.

I was always puzzled by that section in the Bible where Christ asks, "Who is my mother?" Then I understood. He was setting himself free of the role of "son of Mary" (with all the issues that accompany being a good Jewish son) to take on his greater role of "son of God." You see, each role we play is a bundle of beliefs and a bagful of expectations, and when those beliefs and expectations aren't met by others or the world, we're disappointed and take it personally. When we let go of our roles, we can do what we're called to do. We no longer take the world personally or need to make sure that our ego gets attention and validation.

The following is a very powerful exercise that I do with my students to help them let go of their roles.

Exercise: Burning Your Roles

You are reading this book at the level of jaguar, using your mind to understand its language and ideas. This exercise will happen at the level of hummingbird—at the level of the sacred—and the goal is to unravel the energetic cords that keep you bound to a particular role. This exercise is best done in silence by a fire, but you can also do it lighting a candle indoors. You'll also need toothpicks, a pen, and strips of paper.

First, on each strip of paper, write the name of a character you play in your life. Be sure to include at least 20 roles, including *mother, son, father, provider, nurse, healer, recovering alcoholic, lover, sympathetic friend, poet, person who is trying to quit smoking,* and any others you find. Then wrap each piece of paper around a toothpick, and use your breath to "blow" into it your intention to release that role. Then hold the toothpick to the fire and watch it burn. Hold each burning stick in your fingers as long as you possibly can without getting singed. As each wrapped stick is blazing, imagine that you release the future of that character until it's extinguished, until you're no longer mother, son, man, or woman. In doing so, you'll unravel the energetic cords that keep you bound to that character.

I did this exercise when my son was in his early teens, and one of the characters I incinerated was that of father. As the stick was smoldering, I said to myself, "I am placing in the fire who I expect you to be, son, so that you can become who you came in this world to be." Our relationship since then has always been that of friends, although he knows that I am always there for him.

New and Better Stories

The best reason to shed your stories, like a snake sheds its skin, is because you can never heal yourself within your story. You can only resign yourself to accept the lot in life ascribed to you in the script, and then doom yourself to the suffering written into the drama. Your aging mother will never stop being devious, and your ungrateful children will continue to ignore you. But when you craft an epic story for yourself, healing and transformation happen at the level of hummingbird and trickle down to inform your psychological and physical world.

If you're going to spin yarns about your life journey, you might as well make them grand, ennobling ones. It's better to see yourself as a brave traveler who made a harrowing, narrow escape that taught her to trust her instincts than to see yourself as a victim of betrayal who lost everything of value to some cruel persecutor and now cannot bring herself to trust men.

None of your stories are true—they're just scripts you've created. They are not your life, because they keep you living in the past, stuck in a scripted role of misunderstood son, underappreciated artist, or victim of chronic illness. Even the empowering tales you'll learn to spin and use to replace the old, oppressive ones will still be mere trail maps. They'll help you navigate through life and climb the mountain, but they're not the mountain itself.

When you understand the first insight and follow its four practices, you'll gradually shed your identification with ego and find it easier to let go of your stories. Instead of searching for meaning and purpose at the literal level, you will find it at the mythic level, where the stories are epic and sacred. When this happens, you will die to who you've convinced yourself you are and become a mystery unto yourself. You will no longer ask the question "Who am I?" but instead will wonder "*What* am I?" and realize that you're made of the stuff of stars, that you are God appearing in the form of yourself. You're so much larger than your stories, and you have so much to discover about your potential.

For example, a woman I know learned that when she was an infant, her mother (who had been overwhelmed at times by the burden of raising two young children) had sometimes fed her by propping a bottle in her mouth instead of cradling her and holding the bottle. I had to wonder how this fact had changed the woman's perception of her mother: The day before, she hadn't known this information, and today, she knew it. Her mom was the same person she'd been on the previous day. Yet the woman was convinced that this discovery revealed that she'd been harmed in some way, so she felt depressed and betrayed. She dearly wished she hadn't learned this fact about her mother. Although she had no evidence that she'd suffered because of this treatment as an infant, she immediately scripted a story in which her cold and abusive parent had mistreated her.

When we shed negative, unoriginal stories, such as "My mother was selfish and neglected me," we can love and accept her as she is. We can stop wishing that our past had been different, obsessing over how things would have turned out if only Mom and Dad had been the parents we wanted them to be. We can appreciate the gifts they were able to give us instead of focusing on those they didn't. Our new, more positive story about an absent father may be a tale of a child who learned the value of independence. We can discard the old story about our grandparents being judgmental and cruel and script a new one about how they taught us that when you *are* judgmental, you end up causing yourself and others pain and misery. In this new tale, we can celebrate the fact that we were taught to value tolerance.

If we wrote stories like these for our lives, we could do away with most psychotherapy.

The Three Archetypal Characters in Our Stories

To begin transforming your wounds into sources of power and compassion, you need to recognize the stories that you tell yourself about who you are. You might be completely unaware of how deeply you believe in these tales. You may get defensive and insist you have a right to hold on to your truth—that you've been victimized, misunderstood, abused, abandoned, betrayed, and so on. But if you're able to let go of your narrative and your limited definitions of yourself, you can change the trajectory of your life, reinvent yourself, and fashion a much more empowering journey for you, your family, and the human race as a whole.

Whenever we tell a story about our experience or that of someone else, we cast the characters in three roles that form an oppressive *triangle of disempowerment.* These characters are the *victim,* the *perpetrator,* and the *rescuer.* In the Native American world, they are the Indian, the conquistador, and the priest. In any dynamic, the Indian represents the victim, who is bullied by the conquistador, who is the perpetrator. The priest functions as the noble rescuer who tries to help the poor Indian with the promise of an afterlife.

Triangle of Disempowerment

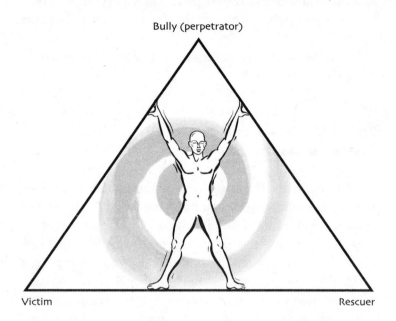

Bully (perpetrator)

Victim

Rescuer

When you live within the script of your story, you create what is known as a *trauma bond* with the leading actors in your tale because you connect with them from your wounded self. In your own stories, you're always acting out one of these roles, although you'll switch characters as the yarn unfolds.

For example, I know a social worker who helps domestic-violence survivors. She used to think of her clients as victims, and she worked overtime to protect these women from the men who abused them. Her behavior had some very positive consequences, because in many instances, she prevented her clients from being further victimized. However, that success came at a great personal cost: Since she had become enmeshed in her rescuer role, she felt hurt and victimized when some of her clients began to resent her paternalistic attitude toward them. And she directed so much rage toward the abusers that she became a perpetrator herself, determined to see these men suffer instead of recognizing that they, too, were in need of healing and may well have been victims of domestic violence themselves when they were children. Unwittingly, the social worker had become caught up in the triangle of disempowerment.

In any situation, healing for all is most likely to occur when someone is able to break out of character and step out of their story. The problem is that we expend so much energy acting out these dramas that we become blind to our purpose, unable to achieve any growth. We're not here to continually reenact the unhealed part of our narrative and define ourselves by what happened in the past. We don't have to be nobly rescuing victims, being hurt when they start to resent us, and then lashing out at them because we've shifted into the bully role. Yes, it's wonderful to help others, but when we're doing it in order to fix the unhealed part of ourselves, we get stuck in this dramatic triangle and prevent true healing for all.

Eventually, my social-worker friend became conscious of being stuck playing the roles of noble rescuer and righteous persecutor. Instead, she started to see the abusive partners as human beings who were on their own journey of healing and was able to let go of her need to watch them all endure punishment.

When you step outside your story, you let go of judgments toward others. For example, when I say, "I feel misunderstood by you," I'm telling you my interpretation of your behavior and suggesting that you're doing something wrong to me. This is a judgment masquerading as a feeling. Outside the story, I could tell you the things that I need instead, such as to be respected and heard. You no longer need to keep another in the character scripted by your yarn—blame for yourself and others falls away, and you can practice forgiveness.

Our Cultural Myths and Stories

When you recognize the narrative that you're trapped in and colluding with, you can decide to let go of it. But first you must recognize the story. This is why the archetypal myths—those tales of gods and heroes—are so valuable. We're able to see our own journeys in them, along with the lessons we must learn in order to transcend them.

Just as we cling to disempowering personal stories, we also buy into larger cultural myths that speak to our need to play the victim, rescuer, or perpetrator. Psychologists say that we act out these characters in our daily lives. We relive the tales of men and women who triumph over adversity, fail because of a fatal flaw in their character, or are rewarded for their sacrifices. We perceive ourselves as suffering like Job or putting forth a Herculean effort.

Even those who are unaware of the archetypal stories unconsciously identify with them. For example, a few years ago some people grumbled quite publicly about all the media coverage of Princess Diana's sudden, tragic death, which seemed to overshadow the saintly Mother Teresa, a woman who had become the very symbol of self-sacrifice and who had died in the same week. They wondered why we should focus so much on a troubled young royal's life when the world had lost someone who would surely be put on the fast track to canonization by the Catholic church.

The answer is that the media responded to the fact that more people identified with Princess Diana than they did with Mother Teresa. In real life, both of these women were complicated people, just like anyone, but we were able to identify with the legend around their lives that most suited our purposes. We wanted to see Mother Teresa as a super-human rescuer whose actions were so out of the ordinary that we couldn't possibly measure up. This way, we could be inspired by her without feeling pressured to follow her example of sacrifice, compassion, and love, which seemed too grand for us to grasp (even though Mother Teresa herself said, "God has created us so we do small things with great love").

Princess Diana, on the other hand, seemed all too human: She innocently believed in her older husband, only to be betrayed by him; she was generous, thoughtful, and compassionate, yet her mother-in-law disapproved of her; and she fell into the depths of despair, bulimia, and depression. However, she rose from her victimhood like the phoenix and become a wonderful mother and a selfless advocate for the less fortunate, such as land-mine victims and AIDS patients.

Many people aspired to be as resilient as Diana seemed to be. The facts of her life (and death) were less important to most than the grand, redemptive myth of a woman who claimed her power, ceased being a victim, and never became bitter or selfish. The myth created around her felt more intimate than the one created around Mother Teresa. Thus, to many, her loss felt more personal.

When we look at stories in the media, we see ourselves. We identify with characters in movies, celebrities who carefully hone their public images, and ordinary people on reality-television shows whose sagas have been directed and edited by professionals who know how to construct a narrative thread that will attract or repel us. We don't really want to know that the rock star or TV actor featured in the *Where Are They Now?* documentary is angry and bitter because his glory days are behind him. We want him to participate in our common belief that when the mighty fall, they reinvent themselves, discover a new purpose, and are happier than they ever dreamed possible.

Even though we're usually unaware of them, these repackaged myths have become addictive for us. The story of Princess Diana is a version of the Greek myth of Psyche and her search for Persephone's beauty cream (that is, happiness), which takes her on a journey to the underworld. The story of Donald Trump is a polished version of the myth of Parsifal and the quest for the Holy Grail, along with his failure to adhere to the admonition to never seduce, or be seduced by, a fair maiden.

The problem is that these ancient cultural myths are no longer supportive or productive for today's world. Rather, they keep us stuck in victimhood, as rescuers, in angry self-righteousness, or in illusions about ourselves that we're afraid to examine because we fear that we'll be exposed as frauds or failures. When we're unable to rise from our own ashes, we fall into despair.

Our healing journey can't progress if we don't discard these old myths and resist the temptation to relive the same tired old stories that we've been hearing for millennia. We need to walk away from all that we thought we were supposed to do or be in order to be loved and accepted by others. We then become the actor instead of the reactor, the mythmaker instead of the myth perpetuator. We bring the sacred to every moment and render our experiences epic.

You can do this when you recognize that every story is a self-fulfilling prophecy. You can tell your tale in such a way that you reclaim your nobility and power . . . in a way that has never been told before. This is the hero's journey.

Cast Out of the Garden

All of us have internalized our culture's Judeo-Christian story of being cast out of paradise, when we were separated from our divine Creator. This bankrupt story permeates our lives whether we were raised in a religious home or not, causing us a great deal of suffering. So if we wish to heal our wounds on every level, it's crucial that we discard this myth and come up with a new one.

This legend is the "original story," featuring the serpent and Eve as perpetrators, Adam as victim, and the grace of God as the only power that will rescue them (and us). Because we buy into this story, we baptize babies, lest they suffer punishment for the stain of original sin that they were supposedly born with. And the sin of our original mother gives rise to *all* of our mother complexes: Perhaps if only Eve had been the right kind of mother and thought more about us instead of thinking about herself, we wouldn't be in the predicament we're in today. Finally, the myth of God as rescuer keeps us separate from our own divinity, causing us to depend on an outside force to deliver us from the curse cast upon us as punishment for the sins of our ancestors.

When we free ourselves from the old myth of the fall from grace, we're able to rediscover the original Eden in nature and feel comfortable in that home. We've been conditioned to think of the natural world as beautiful and awe inspiring but frightening (unlike the protected, cultivated Garden of Eden). As children we were taught that the forest is filled with witches and tricky wolves who prey on little girls. As adults we believe that the great outdoors is populated by violent animals who would tear us limb from limb in an instant; and that Mother Nature is fickle and cruel, randomly attacking us with tidal waves, lightning storms, earthquakes, and tornados that violently snatch our loved ones away from us. We see nature as something to be conquered and tamed, like a well-pruned bush or meticulously manicured lawn.

When we let go of this story, we discover that we never left the Garden of Eden. While we may believe that God created nature, we don't believe that divinity resides within the trees, the oceans, or the cliffs. We conceive of God as an entity far above us, residing in heaven and coming into our hearts only if we issue an invitation and truly humble ourselves, admitting to our many sins. Or we don't believe in the divine at all and can't imagine that the sacred might be present in every leaf, sidewalk, and drop of water. We scoff at the notion that we're already in paradise.

In fact, most people don't realize that despite all those exquisite paintings of a celestial heaven that fill our museums and inspire the imagination, Jesus actually said that the kingdom of heaven is all around us right now. Similarly, the Laika believe that the kingdom of heaven is within and without—inside us, above us, below us, and all around us—it's our inability to perceive it that makes us outcasts, and this blindness causes us to suffer. When the missionaries first told the Laika that underneath the earth is where we will find hell, they were baffled. To them the earth was the domain of the Great Mother, whose fertile land and waters provided food and sustenance to all people, so only a deranged person would embrace the illusion that we're distant from the sacred garden we were born into.

We're still living in the lush garden of the divine, but understanding this intellectually, from jaguar, isn't enough. If we're to experience it as a paradise, we have to feel this in every cell and bone in a sacred way, from the level of hummingbird. The Laika call this *ayni,* or right relationship to nature. When we are in ayni, we don't have to fear nature. It's only when we're out of balance that we may be killed by a lightning bolt, a panther, or a microbe—in fact, for the Laika, there's no difference between being killed by a panther or by a microbe. In the West, we tend to think that one death is caused by a disease and the other by an accident, but the Laika believe we have to be in right ayni with both panthers and microbes or they'll both be looking at us as lunch. When we're in ayni, we're no longer part of their food chain.

In fact, Earthkeeper medicine practices are based on the idea that we must realign ourselves with nature and come back into balance, and then our natural health will return. This is very different from the Western view of the body as a system that inexplicably goes awry and needs to be fixed with operations and antibiotics that kill microbes when it doesn't function at an optimal level.

When we're in ayni, paradise is our home; and physical, mental, and emotional health is our birthright. We discover that we never left Eden. Once, many years ago, I was walking near the Amazon River with a couple of shamans, and we reached a clearing. They told me to walk across the grass and into the jungle to see what would happen. As I crossed the meadow and stepped into the rain forest, I heard its song: the chatter of the macaws, the parrots, the monkeys, and the insects. I took the first step, then the second, and on the third step, the jungle grew quiet. I couldn't believe it.

The shamans explained, "The creatures know that you don't belong here, that you've been kicked out of the garden." I thought that was absurd—surely the animals were smelling the remnants of my deodorant and my athlete's-foot powder, even though I hadn't used any of these for a few weeks.

I then saw two natives cooking a boa constrictor on a spit by the edge of the river, and I got an idea. I approached them, introduced myself, and asked if I could have a little of the snake fat, which they'd been collecting in a tin can. They were happy to oblige.

I returned to my friends the shamans, stripped down to my shorts, and smeared myself with the fat, convinced that the birds, monkeys, and other creatures would smell it on me and think that I was just another serpent slithering back into the rain forest, and thus continue their song. Reeking of boa fat, I confidently took a step into the jungle and then another, yet by the third step, all had grown silent once again. The only difference was that this time I could hear the buzz of about 600 flies swirling around me, attracted by my stench.

Ten years later, after I had learned the ways of the Earth-keepers, I found that when I would stride into the rain forest, the creatures and insects who sensed my presence would recognize me as someone who lived in the garden, and their chattering and squawking and singing would continue uninterrupted even as I delved deep into their realm. They knew that I was someone who walked with beauty on the earth, who belonged with them. I had come to realize that to be in harmony with the garden, I had to drop my story, the cultural myth I'd bought into: that I'd been banished from my original nature, that I could no longer talk to God or the rivers and trees and expect them to answer me. I stopped believing that I was doomed to remain an outcast forever. I'd become the storyteller of my life.

Becoming the Storyteller

The ancient Laika had little use for dogma, including their people's traditional religion, yet they tolerated their native priests, who were the protectors of their culture's stories. They understood that these stories, like our own in the Bible, served to convey the values that held the fabric of society together. However, they didn't hold the old tales in such reverence that they were afraid to explore new ones. They recognized that change is a part of the human experience, and that the mores of a particular time and people can become outdated.

The Laika believe that priests—not just the Spanish priests, but also those of their own native culture—are retellers of stories they did not write, those about another man's experience with the divine. They see religion as simplistic, using narrative to explain spirituality and metaphor to express wisdom. Earthkeepers believe that these stories help us understand certain concepts, but they're not as valuable as experiencing the divine firsthand at the level of eagle perception. They see priests as practicing a kind of theater that makes the immense mystery of creation palatable to the human mind. This is because religion is based on belief, whereas a spiritual practice is based in a personal experience of the divine. The Laika are fiercely focused on developing the wisdom of experience and believe that each one of us must do this on our own. Then the stories we forge become our own sacred tales of epic adventure.

In the following exercise, you'll practice becoming a storyteller by reframing the key events of your life.

Journaling Exercise: Two Stories about Yourself

In this exercise, you'll write two stories. The first is one you've been telling yourself for many years that begins with, "Once upon a time, the stork dropped off a baby at the wrong house." Go ahead and give yourself permission to write the narrative of your life, factoring in the parents, the relationships, the marriage, and the career that didn't work out right. Write this as a fairy tale, as if it had happened to someone in a kingdom long ago, and make note of the times that you were the victim, the perpetrator, and the rescuer, and whom you cast as these same characters.

When you're finished, write the story again, only this time, start it with the words "Once upon a time, the stork dropped off a baby at the *right* house." Remember that healing stories explain why events happened exactly as they were supposed to in order to bring you valuable lessons that would take you farther along on your epic journey.

Perhaps you were abused as a child—but this was just what your soul needed for you to learn the lessons about strength and compassion you required, and you chose the perfect home to be dropped off at. (Of course it's terrible to be abused, but remember that what you're writing here is the story of an epic journey of lessons and healing.) Because your parents were verbally abusive, you may have learned that those who openly disparage others in an attempt to hurt them are deeply insecure and unhappy, and it has nothing to do with you. Maybe you even found a grain of truth in their words. Or perhaps the lesson you gleaned was that you can accept that you're imperfect, and decide just how much effort you want to make to change without feeling pressured to "fix" yourself to meet anyone's expectations.

If you feel uncomfortable writing the story because you haven't learned your lessons yet, that's okay—write it as if you had. You may also wish to come back to it later to shape it further. When you begin to believe this new tale, it will start to come true. You will have become the storyteller of your own life; as a result, the universe, recognizing that you have mastered your lessons, will stop putting you back into the classroom.

In retelling our stories, we uncover the positive, empowering legacy that we've been given. For example, the Laika hold the memory of the conquistador not as a devastating force that destroyed all that was precious in their world (which is the popular view), but as a catalyst for an age in which the Earthkeepers would be especially careful to guard and value the insights. Because these wisdom teachings were hidden, they became even more powerful since there would come a time when they would be expressed again and would be able to help the entire human race survive. The Laika believe that without the conquistadors, we might have become lazy and complacent and allowed the insights to be forgotten.

Remember that we can only rewrite our stories at the mythic level. That is, if you have teenagers whom you'll soon have to put through college, you have to work long hours as a flight attendant to finance it, and you can't spend your day painting watercolors (which is what you'd like to do), those are the facts. However, at the level of the sacred, your story might be that you are an artist, that your canvas is the world, and that everyone you come in contact with in that airplane are people you can touch with a bit more color and life.

Own your mythic story, practice your art, and don't define yourself as only a parent and a flight attendant who is putting her kids through college—you are a painter or poet who happens to have a day job. As you do so, you'll find that time will appear in your day for your art. Acknowledge your inner life, and allow yourself permission to explore who you are in all your wonderful complexity. Bravely embrace your many characters, but don't become any of them. Instead, surprise yourself as your many selves come out from where they've been hiding.

Of course, when you shed your story, those who are invested in your rubber-stamped identity may drift away, unsure of how to relate to the mother who has become an activist or the son who has quit his job in the family business to become a world traveler. If you look to others to encourage you to explore and foster your many selves, you'll probably be disappointed.

We have a hard time embracing the idea that a circuit-court judge can play bass guitar in a rock band, or that a bookkeeper could be a champion dogsled racer. We struggle to accept that our easygoing preteen has become a willful teenager, or that our always upbeat spouse has discovered her quiet and introspective side. But when we break away from our limited ideas about who we are, it becomes easier to acknowledge the artist, the poet, and the mythic traveler in others.

Shedding Our Ancestral and Karmic Stories

When you walk the way of the hero, you cast off the narrative you've inherited, which can go back thousands of years. Your story isn't new—it's a replay of what happened to you in your childhood, which is a retelling of the same plot you've played out over the course of many lifetimes. It's the same tale that drew you to the family you were born into because it dovetailed so well with theirs. It's also the saga you inherited from your mother and father, the one they were unable to heal. You inherit these wounds from your parents and then pass them on to your children, in the hopes that they'll heal them for you. In the Amazon, they call these "ancestral curses."

If you want to get rid of your historical baggage, it's important to honor your ancestors; if you don't, they'll continue living through you and haunting every endeavor and relationship in your life. But if you respect and celebrate them, no matter how awful their legacy, you can move on . . . and so can they. You change your ancestral story and break the curse for them, your children, and your children's children. You won't feel hurt and angry as you remember that your father walked out on your family, or cling to your old story of how that's the reason you feel you can't trust romantic partners.

Karma runs in families. A cold mother raises a child who becomes a smothering mom, who raises a daughter who, as a result of being smothered, doesn't even want children. As each generation attempts to work through the legacy of the family trauma, someone has to make a conscious decision to rewrite the story.

In my family, for instance, my grandfather lost all his money in the Depression when he was 49. My father lost his position, his home, and his career and had to flee Cuba during the Communist revolution when he was 48. When my brother was 49, he lost his life. When I was 48, the so-called family curse—the karma that my father and grandfather had suffered from—struck me. I went through a very difficult time during which my spouse and I separated and she took our children to live in another state. I lost my home and my family; I was reliving the fate of my father and his father before him.

Then one day, while hiking alone in the Andes, I was startled by a familiar whisper. I believed I heard my father's voice telling me, "Until you realize why you were born my son, you will continue living my life." This launched me into a two-year exploration of my family's history, where I discovered this pattern of catastrophic loss. Then I went back to my father's message and understood that I'd made a punctuation error. What he was trying to tell me was, "Until you realize *why you were born,* my son, you will continue living my life." I was then able to thank him for his wise counsel and no longer hold him responsible for my fate. My task was to realize what I came to learn in this life—in the process, I became the author of my own story. I no longer had to unknowingly live my father's life all over again and continue making the same mistakes he and his father had made. Moreover, my own son had been freed from the "family curse" altogether.

When we rewrite our story, we elevate our ancestors from the gutter, no longer holding them responsible for our lives, and we break the negative legacies they've handed down to us. We let go of stories such as "I'm a neurotic mess because my mother was completely crazy" or "I'm angry and misunderstood, just like my father and his father before him." We're no longer victims of the folly of our ancestors—instead, we can honor them and thank them for their gifts, no matter how painful it was to receive them.

Exercise: **Building Your Ancestral Altar**

Most anthropologists still believe that the ancestral altars found in every traditional culture are used for "worship." The truth is that these societies understand that when you celebrate your ancestors, no matter how terribly they might have behaved, you find forgiveness and compassion and can break free of their karma and stories. The Laika say that if you don't honor the ancestors with an altar you build for them, they will run amok in your house. That is, it's better to know where they are than to ignore their legacy, kick them into the psychological gutter, and cling to the story of being a victim of their actions.

The following exercise can spare you from spending years in psychotherapy working through your mother and father issues:

Find a spot in your home (such as a shelf, windowsill, or fireplace mantel) where you can make a small altar, and then place a cloth on it. Next, arrange photographs or symbols of your ancestors on top. For example, if you don't have a picture of your great-grandfather, you might put his ring or some other object he owned on the altar. You can also use slips of paper with your ancestors' names or photographs of homes where your parents, grandparents, or great-grandparents were raised.

I have a friend who created an altar with a runner her great-grandmother embroidered, on which she set a photograph of her grandmother, who was always her inspiration. She also wanted to recognize and honor the ancestors who taught her lessons that caused her pain, but it was very difficult for her to gaze at photographs of them. So she discovered that it was easier to honor them when she placed on her altar photographs of them taken when they were children. Seeing her family members in their youth reminded her of the goodness within them, which had not always been so obvious to her when they were adults.

To honor your ancestors, place fresh flowers in a vase on your altar, or light incense. You may also want to bring your family members offerings from nature as the seasons change, such as shells or stones you pick up from the beach in summer, pinecones and dried leaves in the fall, and so on. Every time you change the offerings, thank your ancestors for the gifts they gave you, no matter how harsh it was for you to experience receiving them or how difficult it was to perceive them as gifts at all. Remember that history is not what actually happened but how you choose to remember it—that is, how it lives within you. Working with this ancestral altar, you can change your family story at the mythic level, where tales are epic journeys, not the same old tired sagas of emotional or material success or failure.

Make a habit of stopping at your altar to reflect upon the gifts of your ancestors. Remember that you've chosen to rewrite your story, and in your revised version, your family members are not villains and you're not a victim.

Keep in mind, too, that this altar must be a representation of the one you build inside of you. That is, what you create in your home should serve as a sort of spiritual Post-it note, reminding you to feel gratitude for the legacy you've been given and the lessons your ancestors taught you.

Attaining Ayni

When we drop our dreary stories of victim, rescuer, and perpetrator, we become storytellers and mythmakers and are provided for in every way. We no longer have to live in fear because we're no longer the victim of our ancestral or cultural stories about scarcity, intimacy, aging, or creativity. Regardless of what we own, we go from scarcity to abundance, from having been cast out of Eden to walking with beauty on the earth. We see what everyone else sees but think something different about it. We become like the lilies of the field, who neither toil nor spin but have all that they need. We may still have to punch a time card, but we can live the life of the artist or poet, with many creative resources available to us.

Many of the indigenous Americans I've met only have a bowl of corn soup on their table for dinner, but they're deeply generous and aware of the abundance in their lives. Once I asked my Earthkeeper mentor, "How can you live in such poverty?" After all, he resided on a mountaintop far from the amenities of city life, and his possessions could have fit in a small closet in a U.S. home. Don Antonio looked at me, puzzled, and then swept his hand over the landscape, at the snowcapped mountains and the rivers below, as if to say, "These are my riches. Which one of us is the poor one?"

On the other hand, I know a very wealthy man who is deeply fearful of losing his money, doesn't have good relationships and is estranged from his children, and trusts no one because he assumes that people only want to be with him so that they can access his money. He's caught up in trying to protect his wealth. He'll offer money to some people in order to feel good about himself, then become offended and feel victimized if they don't take it—or even if they do, but choose to use it differently from how he wanted them to use it. He's resentful and suspicious and lives in a state of scarcity, never experiencing peace or abundance.

The four key practices that follow make up the way of the hero and bring you freedom from your story. They are the practices of nonjudgment, nonsuffering, nonattachment, and beauty.

The Practice of Nonjudgment

To practice nonjudgment, we must transcend our limited beliefs, even the ones about what we think is right and wrong.

We make sense of our world by judging situations as "right" or "wrong" or "good" or "bad," according to rules defined by our culture, which we know as our moral code. But an Earthkeeper is amoral—note that she is not *im*moral, she is simply not ruled by mores. She believes that it's important to let go of these sorts of judgments and maintain her ability to discern.

You see, when you practice nonjudgment, you refuse to automatically go along with others' opinions of any situation. In doing so, you begin to acquire a sense of ethics that transcends the mores of our times. This is important today when the images of the media have become more convincing than reality, and our values—liberty, freedom, love, and the like—are reduced to sound bites and empty platitudes.

When you refuse to collude with the consensual, you have a different perspective. You find what freedom means for you personally, not what was delivered to you by a politician in a well-rehearsed speech. You discover that freedom is more than being able to choose a particular SUV or item from a menu.

Our judgments are assumptions that are based in what we've learned and been told. For example, most of us collude in the belief that cancer is always a deadly disease, so if our doctor says we have it, we immediately become terrified of that "c word." Yet when we practice nonjudgment, we reject the automatic belief that this means we're going to have to battle for life. We may agree to undergo the treatment our physician recommends, but we don't accept that we have a 99 or 1 percent chance of recovery. We don't label our chances of survival "good" or "bad" or place a number on them, because that would be turning our fate over to statistics. Instead, we deal with the problem at hand, not just from the literal level of our body, but from the highest level of perception we can. We allow ourselves to embrace the unknown, along with its unlimited possibilities.

A few years ago, for instance, a friend of mine was diagnosed with prostate cancer. Fortunately, he was living with a healer at the time, who told him, "You don't have cancer—your x-ray just shows unusual spots that we will heal." Within a month, they were indeed able to heal those unusual spots.

Had my friend labeled those spots as "cancerous" and woven a story around them, he would have become a "cancer patient." If he had colluded with this literal story about his illness, he would have been doomed to become a statistic—in his case, one of the 40 percent who heal or the 60 percent who don't. His possibilities would have collapsed into probabilities, for he wouldn't have been able to imagine himself in the 40 percent who heal because he would have been so aware of the odds against him. This is why I teach my students to try to work with clients *before* they get their biopsy results, before the spots on the x-ray get labeled and the "deadly cancer" story can be written in the client's mind and become a self-fulfilling prophecy.

Recently, a woman named Alyce called to schedule a personal consultation with Marcela, who is on our healing staff. Alyce's doctor had performed a mammogram and found a lump in her breast. Marcela asked her if she wanted to work before the biopsy to try to influence the results, or later, in which case they would work with the results of the biopsy. Alyce decided to go for option number one. The following week, she received a call from her doctor's office: She was told that they'd made a mistake and had confused her mammogram for someone else's, and that she had nothing wrong with her breast! So our stories not only influence how we feel about things, but the "real" world out there as well—in this case, healing an event that had already happened!

We can always craft a mythic story around our journey, one that will help us grow, learn, and heal. Ultimately, we may not be able to alter the spots on the x-ray, but we just might heal our souls and finally start learning the lessons we came into this world to get. Our lesson may be to slow down and appreciate the people we have around us; to let go of an existence that we're sleepwalking through because we've become convinced that we're supposed to live our lives a certain way; or, from the perspective of humming-bird, these spots may serve as our wake-up call to make the changes we've been avoiding.

We've created big stories around cancer, HIV, and other diseases, whereas we don't have these stories around other illnesses. If the doctor tells us we have a parasite, for instance, most of us don't think of the millions of people around the world who die of parasitic infections and imme-diately start worrying that we, too, are going to perish. We don't have a story built up around such a malady, even though it *is* often deadly. This is partly because there's little commercial or monetary interest in perpetuating these stories. Treating parasites, although they affect nearly two billion people on the planet, is not big business with big drugs—whereas cancer, cholesterol, and heart disease are. Fear stories sell medications.

When you don't judge the illness or let yourself get stuck in mortal fear that you'll die, you'll find it easier to perceive it from a higher level and write a mythic story. So if you have a parasite, you may recognize it as the literal manifestation of other people's toxic anger that you've internalized and personalized. Alternately, you could realize that you've wandered off your path and are living a life that is poisonous to you.

When we practice nonjudgment, we no longer have illnesses—we have opportunities for healing and growth. We no longer have past traumas—we have events that sharpened our edges and shaped who we are today. We don't reject the facts—we reject the negative interpretation of them and the traumatic story we're tempted to weave around them. We then create a story of strength and compassion based on these facts.

Insight 1 is called the way of the hero because the most effective healers recognize that they were once deeply wounded themselves, and as a result of their own healing, they've developed compassion for others who are hurting. Eventually, their wounds were transformed into gifts that allowed them to feel more deeply and show more compassion. In other words, who better to help an alcoholic break through his denial than someone in recovery who recognizes the lies that a substance abuser will tell himself, and who knows the courage it takes to overcome an addiction? Who better to help a sullen, angry teenager than an

adult whose own adolescence was marked by rebelliousness, resentment, and insecurity, but who has since healed
himself? When someone has "been there, done that," it's
easier for her to let go of judgments and labels and focus
on healing.

The Practice of Nonsuffering

The next practice is that of nonsuffering, which means
not writing stories about our pain. Here we make ourselves
available to learn directly from the infinite wisdom of the
universe—we no longer have to endure the same misfor-
tunes again and again. However, it's imperative that we do
learn our lessons, or we'll end up perpetuating our own
misery. In the East, this is known as breaking the cycle of
karma and stepping into dharma, while the Laika call it
practicing "bliss."

Suffering happens when you wrap a story around the
facts. At some point, you're going to lose a parent, a romantic partner, or a job, so you can spin this fact into as dramatic a yarn as you wish. For example, you can tell yourself,
"Now I'm left motherless, with no one to look after me."
This will become a huge tale, and others will see you as
walking under the sign of the motherless child.

Often we decide how big our story should be by taking a cue from others, in the same way that when a small
child falls down, he instantly looks up at his mother, as if to
ask, "How upset should I be? Was this a bad fall?" He then
creates a story that fits the intensity of her reaction. By the
same token, we surround ourselves with friends who will
sympathize with us; however, in doing so, we allow them
to collude in our story of victimhood, and even enhance it.

They may tell us that we ought to be more than just irritated at our situation, we should be furious! Or they might say that we deserve to feel absolutely awful or deeply resentful. Either way, with their encouragement, we script a dramatic story of being taken advantage of, mistreated, and misunderstood.

Buddha came to teach us that while suffering is a universal human condition, it isn't necessary. That doesn't mean that pain doesn't exist—it's inevitable because we all have a nervous system that feels fire and loss. As I tell my students, if you want to understand the difference between pain and suffering, try the following: While you're standing under a nice hot shower, turn the faucet toward cold, but do it in two steps. First, lay your hand on the faucet and notice your body recoiling in anticipation—this is *suffering*. Then when you suddenly turn the faucet to cold, what you experience is *pain*. You see, misery and anguish happen when you think about how cold the water is going to be and how much it's going to hurt when you feel it hitting your skin.

When a dentist administers a local anesthetic, he can remove a tooth and we won't feel any pain. However, we'll still experience a sensation of pulling or pressure. We should be able to completely relax, knowing that we aren't aching, but our mind wants to start thinking about the experience: *That's the sound of the drill,* and *He's actually removing my tooth from my mouth!* We get nervous and uncomfortable because we're creating a story around pain that we aren't even feeling.

When you practice nonsuffering, you embrace the facts of your life and the lessons they are there to teach you. If the facts are hurtful, of course you will feel that pain, but don't build it up by escalating the story and telling yourself,

This is devastating. I can't bear the grief of living without my partner because it's far too great. It will destroy me.

After losing someone you love, it's only natural that your feelings of sadness will be triggered now and again. You can experience this sorrow and write a heroic tale that makes the pain an important part of your healing, or you can write a story that results in your remaining trapped as a victim and dooms you to even greater misfortune. You can think, *I loved him so much. He brought so much to my life, and I'm grateful for that. I really enjoyed having that kind of a relationship with another human being, and I'd like to have a relationship like that again.* Or you can keep telling yourself, *I can't believe he died. It's so unfair. I'll never get over this.* As you've learned, every story is a self-fulfilling prophecy. The first story promotes healing, while the second promotes suffering. Once you let go of suffering, you can stop learning your lessons through traumas, conflicts, and bad luck—and you can begin to learn directly from knowledge itself.

The Practice of Nonattachment

To practice nonattachment, we let go of the roles we've bought into and the labels we've stuck to ourselves. While our new stories can be far more interesting and productive for us than the old ones were, our goal is to stop identifying with any story whatsoever. We then become self-referencing—that is, we no longer need a fable to define or discover who we are. Even the archetypal tales of the gods and goddesses of old no longer apply to us, for in the end, their legends are tragic, too. When we shed all of our stories, with their limiting roles and confining identities, and become a mystery unto ourselves, we're practicing nonattachment.

For many years, my identity in the world has been "shaman-healer-anthropologist." That's a convenient way for the world to perceive me, but that's not who I really am—I'm much bigger and broader than that. As Walt Whitman once wrote: "Very well then, I contradict myself / (I am large, I contain multitudes)." A few years ago, I became attached to a characterization of myself that appeared in my earlier books, that of the explorer. In a book review, *The New York Times* had even referred to me as the "Indiana Jones of anthropology." I so identified with this character that it became very limiting and one-dimensional.

When I turned 40, the young-anthropologist typecasting became ridiculous, and the rugged adventurer in me was quite exhausted. By rejecting this definition of myself, I was able to open up to other sides of who I was. I discovered that while I'll always be learning, for instance, I'm also a teacher, and now I train others in the medicine way. The adventures I pursue today are of the spirit and are no longer in the deep Amazon.

We all have convenient labels that the world attaches to us to describe how we're primarily perceived: *soccer mom, social activist, recovering alcoholic, vice president, assistant,* and so on. The trouble starts when we believe that the label encompasses all that we are and dictates how we must be. We think that we're supposed to have a certain set of interests, beliefs, and behaviors if we're to be Indiana Jones; and we become confused, embarrassed, or frustrated when we find ourselves thinking, feeling, and operating in a completely different way.

In many spiritual traditions, in order to become a monk or a nun you have to shed your nice clothes, shave your head, and don a simple and cheap robe so that you won't be perceived by anyone as a person of any importance. You're forced to find your reference point internally instead of externally. No one knows who your parents were, what you've accomplished, or what your childhood friends think of you. You get past the ego, or personality, and discover the self that can't be so easily defined. You let go of your attachment to the material and the psychological—and even the spiritual, if you were really devoted to dogma—and your reference point is no longer your ego but your divinity. You detach from the labels you've created for yourself or that you allowed to be created for you.

Nonattachment requires you not only to let go of your roles and your stories, but to also let go of the part of yourself that identifies with these dramas. When you stop attaching your ego to the small identity of a spouse, child, student, teacher, and the like, you let go of your preconceived notions about who you are, and you stop fretting about whether you're pleasing or displeasing others. You stop needing validation from people and becoming upset or sad when you don't receive it. You're free to simply be whoever you want to be.

The Practice of Beauty

To practice beauty is to perceive loveliness even when there's ugliness. For example, instead of thinking of a co-worker as an endless complainer who makes the workplace unbearable, we can perceive him from the level of hummingbird and recognize that he's a perfect symbol of our need to learn how not to personalize other people's unhappiness. When he comes into our cubicle to tell us that we left out a detail in a report, insisting that the document is a disaster and he'll have to rewrite it, we recognize that he's our teacher. And while our minds will always tell us, *What a jerk,* we remember what we're meant to learn: not to overreact to criticism, not to become defensive, to remain centered instead of getting ourselves upset just because someone else is fuming—and that we no longer need to learn from jerks. Then we can bring beauty to the moment by smiling . . . and after that, we can examine why we're in a classroom with the slow learners!

"Beauty before me, beauty behind me, beauty all around me"—these words come from a Navaho prayer of gratitude, from a person who sees only beauty in the world. In other words, we must notice what is pleasant in unexpected places, and bring gorgeousness to where there is hideousness and ugliness. For example, I recently went to an exhibit and saw paintings by an artist who was fascinated by dark alleyways. His paintings of places we usually associate with fear, danger, dirt, and loneliness were alive with energy, bursting with color and pattern. When he painted, he clearly was practicing beauty.

Instead of looking for ugliness and poverty, perceive the beauty all around you. Bring flowers home from work. Say a gracious word to a colleague. Uplift a friend. When you check the departure list at the airport and see that all flights to your destination have been canceled due to bad weather, resulting in your spending Thanksgiving in the airport, you can get angry or you can raise your level of perception and perceive the beauty of the moment. The people you're going to spend time, commiserate, and laugh with at the airport are going to help you create a memorable Thanksgiving if you allow it to be so. So perceive the beauty in that (and any) situation, and find the gift from Spirit. When you see beauty all around you, beauty will seek and find you, even in the most unexpected places . . . and you'll be well on your way to becoming a hero.

INSIGHT 2

The Way of the
Luminous Warrior

———————————◼︎———————————

To be a luminous warrior is to discover the power of fearlessness.

During the time of the Conquest, there was a group of Laika warriors who were dreaded by the Spanish. Legend has it that they could not be killed—even when the conquistadors fired their muskets at them at close range, the bullets would simply miss their mark.

These Laika warriors were the samurai of the Americas, and they believed that if fear lived within you, then you were already as good as dead. The bullet you dreaded would find you. However, if you became a luminous warrior, you could go into battle and avoid defeat. You wouldn't have any enemies who hated and were out to kill you; you'd only have adversaries who, for reasons that had nothing to do with you, may have been aiming a gun in your direction.

When these Laika would slay a particularly honorable opponent, they would shed some of their own blood on the earth because they recognized that at any other time in history, they and the one they killed might be sharing stories around a fire. It's not that these warriors didn't experience being scared, but they weren't moved by fear. Their love radiated so strongly that there was no place for darkness within them, nor for dwelling on what might happen. They lived free in the light of fearlessness, and because of that, they could not be found by death.

When we become luminous warriors, we recognize that our job is to use love to vanquish its opposite—and its opposite is not hate, but fear. Fear is the absence of love in the same way that darkness is the absence of light. Fear disconnects us from Spirit, from nature, and from our own inner selves. Our challenge is to exorcise the fear and its darkness within by embracing love and its light. The second insight teaches us to wield a sword of light and dispel fear forever.

I like to think of *fear* as an acronym for *false evidence appearing as real*—that is, when we focus on what we dread, we give power to false evidence and make it reality. We forget that fear can't be remedied by understanding why we're afraid, just as hunger can't be remedied by understanding why we feel famished. This is why most therapies that focus on helping us understand the origins of our fear are so ineffective at getting us to let go of that fear forever and heal ourselves.

We often confuse love for a warm glow we sense in our bellies and as something we can offer and withdraw, like a cat who comes and goes at its pleasure. It's easy for us to extend love toward those who are lovable, but loving people and situations that are not to our liking isn't so easy. We give our love "unconditionally," but when we don't receive what we feel we deserve, we withdraw it. We then reinvest our love in a new person or situation that we think will give us a better return, but we find it difficult to maintain when we don't feel recognized or acknowledged. If things don't work out the way we want them to, we too readily exchange our loving feelings for hatred and resentment. Our initial excitement over a new job, for instance, may sour and become disappointment and bitterness. When we've been jilted by a lover, the intense, starry-eyed passion of infatuation can turn into loathing so great that it consumes us.

To an Earthkeeper, love is not a feeling or something you barter with. Love is the essence of who you are, and it radiates from you as a brilliant aura: You become love, practice fearlessness, and attain enlightenment.

From Darkness to Light

Buddha showed us the way of illumination and taught us to follow our light so that we may attain freedom from suffering. Christ was surrounded by a blinding radiance when he was baptized in the Jordan River. And Andean storytellers recall the Inka Pachacuti, considered to be a child of the sun, who sparkled with the light of the dawn. These teachers left us with the message that we're capable of even greater things than they—we, too, can access this light and banish the darkness in our lives.

While the light of love versus the darkness of fear may simply sound like a metaphor or the stuff of mythology, there actually is a scientific basis to this universal idea. Scientists know that every living thing on Earth is made of light: Plants receive light from the sun and turn it into life, and animals eat green plants that feed on light. Light is the fundamental building block of life, and we are made up of light that is bound into living matter. Moreover, biologists have discovered that all living cells emit photons of light at the rate of 100 flashes per second. The source of this photon emission is DNA.

Just as the light of love is real, so is the darkness of fear that is stored in every cell of our bodies, perhaps even clouding the light of our DNA. The false evidence that we perceive as real is strong enough to obscure our every thought and affect our every interaction. It feeds upon itself and can begin to defy rationality, as we worry endlessly about what mishaps might befall us.

Fear creates a dark reality. As we learned earlier, every prophecy is self-fulfilling—whatever scares us the most will be waiting for us around the corner. There's nothing wrong with being cautious, but fearfulness holds us back from growing and keeps us repeating our lessons through suffering and trauma instead of through the experience of our own radiance.

Fear denies and distorts our luminous nature. Fearlessness, which is the core practice of the luminous warrior, allows us to experience our light and our illumination.

Stuck in the Fear Response

Fright, or the startle response, is part of a system that allows us to react instinctively to danger. Fright is different from fear and does serve a purpose to ensure our survival, ideally washing right through us once the danger has passed. Our instincts are designed so that in a state of extreme stress, our fight-or-flight response kicks in: Our glands pump adrenaline into our bloodstream, making our blood-sugar levels rise so that we have the energy to put up our dukes or flee the danger.

I'm reminded of the time I saw an antelope in a game reserve in Africa as she was being chased by a lioness. In her attempt to flee, she came to a pond, hesitated for a moment, and then darted over the shallows. I turned to see a crocodile leap out of the water like a torpedo, just missing the doe. Once safely on the other side, she shook from head to tail for a few moments and then went back to grazing calmly. Animals naturally readjust their nervous system to its normal calm-but-alert state after a stressful event; unfortunately, humans lose our ability to quickly pull ourselves out of the startle response.

The *Moro reflex,* which is found in newborn infants, shows how this natural ability to shake off fright works. This reflex is best observed when the baby is faceup on a cushion, and her head is gently lifted. If you suddenly release her head and allow it to flop backward for a moment before quickly supporting it again, the infant will fling her arms out sideways with her palms up. As the reflex ends, the infant will draw her arms back toward her body and then relax and quiver slightly. Unfortunately, the Moro reflex diminishes in humans after the first few months of life.

Fright is instinctual, whereas fear is a learned response. We learn that "men are dangerous" or that "relationships are unsafe." Our feelings trigger our fight-or-flight instinct— yet at the same time, we try to inhibit it because we long for intimacy. It's like flooring the accelerator while slamming on the brakes.

The problem is that we live in a constant state of paralyzed fight-or-flight. We're stuck in a traffic jam, frustrated that we can neither move nor take out our aggression on the idiot in front of us. We come home from a long day at work and a harried commute and snap at our partner or the kids because of something that happened at the office. We're continually on red alert, adrenaline coursing through us, because of our nonstop stress. We no longer have the ability to shake it off, like the antelope or the newborn. As a result, cortisol is released into our bloodstream and wreaks havoc on our organs and cells.

There's nothing as lethal to our organs as high levels of cortisol, a substance that's toxic to the brain. Besides destroying neurons, this steroid hormone upholds the neural pathways that "replay the tapes" of past events that caused us distress. Once the antelope is out of danger and has shaken off its fright, it goes back to grazing peacefully. But once *we* are out of danger, we continue rerunning the events in our mind, thinking about how they might have turned out differently if we'd only been stronger, tougher, or more aggressive; or if we'd only held our ground. This is because the human brain is unable to differentiate between a real stressor (such as someone saying something offensive to you) and a recalled one (such as replaying the tape of the last time you were verbally assaulted). The brain responds to both real and imagined stressors by triggering the fight-or-flight response.

◈

I remember the first time I did a vision quest alone in the jungle. I was up all night, convinced that every sound I heard, each snapping of a branch, was evidence that a jaguar was stalking me. Now, I knew in my head that jaguars in the rain forest are absolutely silent, and I wouldn't have heard one even if it had been right next to me. But my fear won the best of me, and I was unable to enjoy the beauty of that first night alone under the stars by the Mother of

God River. I was too young then to recognize that all my fear was just the false evidence I confused for reality.

Even when you do your best to manage stress, you tend to click into that fight-or-flight state far too often. Think of how your heart races and your breath becomes shallow as you look for your temporarily misplaced wallet or keys. Or consider how anxious you feel when watching a local investigative-news story on how a nearby nuclear-power plant is an easy target for a terrorist attack, or how some new and especially horrible and deadly virus is certain to be diagnosed any day now. All of us are so used to taking in this kind of anxiety-provoking information over the course of sorting the mail or eating dinner that we don't realize that we're having a chemical and physiological reaction to it.

Medically, this is known as an *exaggerated startle response:* Our sympathetic nervous system kicks in, triggering the dumping of adrenaline, cortisol, and sugar into the bloodstream, but the relaxation response doesn't follow. We can't shake off the perceived danger, and even after the initial stress has subsided somewhat, we remain in a state of alert. In fact, this is one of the symptoms of post-traumatic stress disorder (PTSD). PTSD is usually long lasting; in fact, many World War II veterans in their 80s still experience it. In our Healing the Light Body School, I teach students how to disengage the fight-or-flight system, which may have been turned on 40 years ago when they were nearly hit by a car while riding a bicycle.

You see, when our warning system is locked in the *on* position, it creates an energetic band over the second chakra, speeding it up and overworking our adrenal glands (the second chakra is associated with the adrenals and adrenaline production). When we release this energy band, we can reset the second chakra so that instead of spinning at 100 miles an hour, it pulsates to the gentle rhythm of the heartbeat.

I remember helping one of our students, a physician who worked in an emergency room, to decouple this energy band. Afterward, he told me that he was able to relax deeply for the first time in years, but he was concerned about whether or not he'd be able to perform under the high pressure of the ER. He'd become so used to being in a perpetual fight-or-flight response that he couldn't imagine functioning in a relaxed state—yet when he returned to that emergency room, he found he was more focused and productive than he had been when he was fueled by stress.

The Number One Fear

Despite all of our other worries—from losing our money or our job to being rejected by the people we care about—our strongest fear is of annihilation, which is even greater than that of death. In fact, it's so powerful that we hold it in our luminous energy field over the course of our many incarnations.

Although we've experienced birth and death many times, the end of life scares us because we consider it a terminal experience. Yes, we're concerned that it will probably involve physical pain and emotional loss as we leave our loved ones, but what we most dread is the annihilation of our ego. The ego will always fight desperately for its existence, as it's terrified of being absorbed into something larger than itself.

When we identify with the ego, we're concerned about its demise, which will occur when we die. But when we identify with our soul—which is not constrained by or subject to the laws of time, and therefore eternal—our fear dissolves. We recognize that the real death is what happens to us when we begin to sleepwalk through life, lost to our destiny, simply existing without really living.

Physical death is inevitable, although the Laika believe that we can influence its circumstances and even determine when and where we'll die. However, spiritual death, or becoming the walking dead, is something we can and must avoid. I believe that this type of "living death" dulls our light and inhibits our DNA's ability to repair the body, causing us to eventually succumb to emotional and physical disease. So while we believe that there are many causes that lead to death, the Laika believe that there is only one cause of our demise—the darkness of fear, which settles in our cells and tissues.

Every year I take a few of my students on an expedition to a mountain in the Andes where the Laika traditionally gather for their rites of initiation. When we get to the base, we each select a stone to carry in our pocket and meditate with while we hike. I ask my students to stop along the way to "breathe" into the stone the memories of how their parents or grandparents died, and I ask them to remember the times in their lives when they personally felt devoid of life. When we reach our destination, a clear and beautiful pool known to the shamans as the Jaguar Lagoon, we perform a ceremony during which we all take our stones and throw them into the water. We do this at the level of hummingbird, to shed the death that's been selected for us by our genes, parents, or lifestyles. We sever the energetic strands that bind us to reliving the way our ancestors lived or died.

I later explain to our expedition members that if we were in a room of 100 people, statistics show that 31 of us would eventually die of heart disease, 24 of us would die of cancer, and only 1 of us would go the way we'd prefer—perhaps in the arms of our beloved at the age of 110 after having great sex! Of course we all want *that* death, but bell curves and probability tell us not to get our hopes up.

Our belief is that we live in a hostile, predatory universe and that death is stalking us at every turn, from invisible microbes to cancers to poisoned food and water. Yes, we'll all experience physical death, and we wonder how and when it will come about. Although we may be unaware of it, each of us has volunteered to expire in a particular way, by choosing to be born into the families we were born into, the genes we inherited when we selected that family, and the lifestyles that we would create for ourselves. While statistician like to point out how everyone around us will die, the good news is that we can break free of probability and the death preselected for us by our genes and our karma.

When we feel that we're being stalked by death, we live in scarcity instead of abundance, and our glass is always half empty. Operating from a place of fear, we buy into the belief that *I've got to look out for me and mine because no one else will.* We lose our faith and stop trusting that Spirit will look after us. We become disconnected from other people, from ourselves, and from the sacred; and we perceive that we're on our own. We forget the great resources available to us when we're in touch with the divine. Perceiving everything from the level of serpent or jaguar, never from that of hummingbird or eagle, we get trapped in our stories—we're either always living in the past and wishing things had been different or focusing on the future and wishing we could control it. We're never fully present in the moment. When we live this way, we become the walking dead.

Shedding the Death That Stalks You

Once you've cast off the death that's been selected for you, you can let go of the many stories that have been assigned to you by your culture, race, gender, and education. Because you change the end point, all the intermediate steps fall away. For example, when you shed the death that awaits a type A overachiever who smokes, drinks, and never exercises, following through with what you need to do in order to be healthy will come naturally because you are no longer headed toward the inevitable heart attack. You'll actually change the end of your life (as you'll learn to do by using the exercises later in this chapter), and this will alter the path you're on. Your future will reach backward like a great hand and pull you in a different, healthier direction.

No longer will you have to struggle unsuccessfully with dieting, exercising, or managing stress (although you'll still have to deal with these issues) because your entire lifeline will have been redirected. If you learn to live as a luminous warrior, you'll know that after death, there's only life. You'll be able to let go of your fear of death and exorcise the lifelessness that has settled into your joints, tissues, and muscles. Your body will be more supple, and vitality will return.

We may know an older person who seems to be in love with life, appearing much younger than some of the world-weary, cynical youths we've met. And we all know people who have been claimed by death little by little so that they're walking around more dead than alive—they are living in a hostile, predatory universe that has to be guarded against and kept at bay all the time. When we recognize that we live in paradise and endeavor to be in ayni, we discover that the universe is not only benign, but that it will actually go out of its way to conspire on our behalf. We feel fully alive and are amazed at how the universe provides for us.

The challenge, then, is to shed your fear and embrace love. The way to do so is to confront your preselected death at the energetic level instead of the literal one—in other words, at the level of eagle, not at that of serpent. You want to face this death as a sacred passage, not as a catastrophic event in the ER. You can experience it and let it go so that it no longer stalks you; and later in this chapter, you'll learn about the practices of fearlessness, nondoing, certainty, and nonengagement, which will allow you to be fully alive, so you can never again be stalked by death.

Facing Infinity from the Level of Eagle

Death at a physical (serpent) level means that your heart stops and your brain waves cease. At the level of mind (jaguar), the result is that you lose your sense of self and realize this is the only time around as "you." At the level of the soul (hummingbird), the death of the body means the beginning of a journey to another family, another body, and another lifetime.

When physical death occurs, there's hardly a disruption: At the level of Spirit, you continue to experience yourself as a being of conscious energy that dwells outside of time. You recognize that you're infinite and that death is simply a change of skin—a transition from one form to the next, a new adventure. As a result, death ceases to be a terminal experience and loses its menace.

After physical expiration, you leave the visible world and enter the invisible one. Your soul returns to the river of the greater consciousness, of Spirit. You retain your memories, but they're in your subconscious so you're unaware of them. These memories are encoded in your eighth chakra and become lodged in your LEF and your body's cells and tissues when you reincarnate.

We can revisit these memories when we do a past-life regression, which the next exercise will accomplish. But we shouldn't get caught up in the stories of our past lives because they're simply more tales, and not so interesting ones at that. Instead, our goal is to help the people we once were to die consciously so that we can release the fear and break the karma of those former lives. We then shed the way that death has continued to fester and linger within us across many incarnations.

The following exercise will allow you to heal the marks these previous deaths left in your luminous matrix, freeing yourself from the mistakes you made back then and from the way death claimed you. You'll accomplish this by journeying to three specific lifetimes to help the self that was once you experience these deaths peacefully. You'll forgive yourself and those around you; coach yourself to take a final, deep, cleansing breath; and follow your soul as it returns back home to the world of Spirit, intact. You'll come to closure with that lifetime by healing the last five minutes of that existence.

When you can transit consciously and without fear through the doorway of death and realize that there's only life, love, and forgiveness on the other side . . . then you don't bring any karma or unfinished business with you. Please keep in mind that while you've lived many lives before this one, you don't need to go back one at a time to clear all of their memories—you only need to work with the three lives that hold the most potent recollections. The rest of your past-life experiences will peel away by themselves, as you no longer have the receptor sites of fear to bind them to you. The lifetimes you'll be working with are the one in which you suffered the most, the one in which you had the greatest power and knowledge but abused it, and the one in which you had the greatest power and knowledge and used it to serve others.

For the Laika, this is not just an exercise in active imagination, for they understand that we can all journey back along our timelines to heal events that occurred in the past. Your former selves will hear an angelic voice telling them that all is forgiven, allowing them to return home in peace. The angel is you reaching back into the past, healing yourself.

EXERCISE: Burning the Karma of Three Former Lifetimes

(Note: Please read through this exercise a few times before you follow it, or record it on a tape recorder so that you can use it anytime you wish.)

Sit comfortably, close your eyes, and bring your hands into a prayer pose at your heart. Very slowly extend your hands up your centerline, past your forehead, so your palms are pressed together above your head. Then reach up to your eighth chakra and expand this radiant "sun" to envelop your entire body, sweeping your arms out to your sides like a peacock unfurling its feathers. You have now opened sacred space.

Bring your hands to rest at your lap. Perform the "little-death exercise," which is done by inhaling to a count of seven, holding your breath for a count of seven, exhaling to a count of seven, and holding your breath out for a count of seven. Do the little death ten times.

Feeling fully relaxed, and continuing to breathe deeply and slowly, imagine yourself in a small box canyon in the desert, surrounded by high red-rock walls. You're sitting on a boulder above a shallow crystalline pool and can see the sandy bottom. Next to you are three colored pebbles: a black stone that will call forth the lifetime in which you suffered the most, a red stone that will allow you to witness the lifetime in which you had the greatest knowledge and power but misused it, and a yellow stone that will reveal the lifetime in which you had the greatest wisdom and power and used it to serve others.

Reach down and hold the black stone firmly in your hand. Squeeze it tightly and then release it into the pool. Observe as it strikes the water, creating ripples in the surface of the pond. Look into the ripples and invite the images of that lifetime to appear. Are you a man or a woman? What color is your skin? What year is this? Are you wearing shoes or sandals, or are you running barefoot? Are you walking on grass or cobblestones? Where do you live? Who is your family? *Where* is your family? Allow this lifetime to unfold before you, observing it but not engaging any of its drama. Spend a few moments visiting this self from long ago.

Breathe deeply and allow yourself to reexperience the last five minutes of that lifetime that was yours but is no longer. Speak to your former self and help him or her to die peacefully. Say, "It's all right, my love. All is forgiven. It's time to come home. Take a final deep breath and set your spirit free."

Observe as a look of peace and serenity comes over the face of that self that was once you, as it releases its final

breath and sets its soul free. Follow the luminous orb of
your soul as it leaves that body and rises above the room
and the house or field you're in, and goes through a dark
tunnel back toward the light of the world of Spirit. As you
emerge into the light, sense how you are welcomed back
home by your luminous parents.

Now observe these images breaking up and dissolving
back into the sands of time at the bottom of this pool, until
the surface is still and crystalline once again. Take a deep
breath and reach for the red stone, which will summon
the lifetime in which you had the greatest knowledge and
power but used it wrongly. Squeeze your hand around the
red stone, release it into the pool, and observe as it strikes
the water. Look into the pool's ripples as the images of your
previous life begin to form. Are you a man or a woman?
What color is your skin? Are you walking on grass or sand
or cobblestones? Do you live in a village or a town? Where
is your family? What year is it?

Continue your observation: How did you grow up?
What were your gifts and talents? Who trained you? How
did you use your knowledge? How did you abuse your
power? What happened to your loved ones? How did you
grow old? Whom did you marry? Who were your children?
How did you die? Who was by your side and held your
hand at your deathbed? Whom did you not forgive? Who
did not forgive you?

Now let yourself reexperience the last five minutes of
that lifetime that was yours but is no longer, speak to your
former self, and help him or her to die peacefully. Again, say,
"It's all right, my love, it's okay. All is forgiven. It's time to
come home. Take a final breath and set your spirit free."

Observe how a look of peace and serenity comes over
the face of that self that was once you, as it releases its final

breath and sets its soul free. Follow the luminous orb of your soul as it leaves that body and rises above the room you're in, and goes through a dark tunnel back toward the light of the world of Spirit, to be welcomed back home by your luminous parents.

Now observe these images breaking up and dissolving back into the sands of time at the bottom of this pool, until the surface is crystalline once again. Take a deep breath, and reach for the yellow stone, the one that will call forth the lifetime in which you had the greatest wisdom and power and used it correctly. Observe as this stone strikes the water, creating ripples in the surface of the pool, and look into the ripples as the images begin to take shape. Are you a man or a woman? What color is your skin? Are you wearing shoes or sandals, or are you running barefoot? Where do you live? What year is it? How did you grow up? What were your gifts? Who taught and trained you? Whom did you serve? *How* did you serve? Whom did you love? What were your talents? How did you grow old? How were you honored? How did you die? Who was by your side when you died?

Now let yourself reexperience the last five minutes of that lifetime that was yours but is no longer, speak to your former self, and help him or her to die peacefully. Tell this self, "It's all right, my love, it's okay. All is forgiven. It's time to come home. Take a final breath and set your spirit free."

Observe a look of peace and serenity coming over the face of that self that was once you, as it releases its final breath and sets its soul free. Follow the luminous orb of your soul as it leaves that body, rises high into the sky, and goes through a dark tunnel back toward the light of the world of Spirit, to be welcomed back home by your luminous parents.

Now observe these images breaking up and dissolving back into the sands of time at the bottom of this pool, until the surface is crystalline once again. Cross your hands over your chest and take three deep breaths. Come back into the room and fully inhabit your body again. Shake your hands vigorously and knead them together. Now rub your face with your hands and open your eyes. Close sacred space by sweeping your arms and gathering your eighth chakra again at the top of your head. Bring your hands back to prayer pose.

JOURNALING EXERCISE:
How You Wish to Be Remembered

Now that you've cleared the lingering deaths of these former lifetimes, you can chart a healed and empowered course for the next leg of your journey here on Earth.

Imagine that you've lived a long and rich life, and now you're on your deathbed. Write your own eulogy, featuring rich detail about how you lived, how you loved, what adventures you went on, how you were of service, and how you wish to be remembered. How did you touch other people? What did you learn? What did you overcome? What meant the most to you?

When you've finished writing this eulogy, you might want to share it with those you love, as it's a road map for the life you are called to live but may not be living. Think about whether you're actually on the road to living this life that you've described; if not, ask yourself what needs to change today.

Divine Will

After we exorcise the deaths that lived within us, we understand that we're capable of changing anything in our lives. No risk is too great, and no endeavor too daunting. When we're no longer motivated by fear, we also understand that every moment is perfect in its own way. We no longer dread that which we can't control, and we learn to respect the wisdom of Spirit rather than impose our will on situations. This is the path of genuine power.

When our relationship to Spirit is no longer colored by fear, we don't need intermediaries to help us contact the divine. We can actually sit across the table from God at dinnertime and boldly yet respectfully ask for what we would like, adding, "and may Thy will be done."

If this direct encounter with the sacred sounds too brash, it's because we're still caught in the victim triangle, perceiving God to be our ultimate rescuer. Many of us have forgotten that our mythology provides us with examples of those who loved God enough to be honest and forthright with Him about what they wanted. For example, in the Bible, God told Abraham that His people had lost their way. He told Abraham to look at Sodom and Gomorrah, cities of sin that He was going to destroy.

Abraham asked God, if he could find 50 righteous men, would He then spare these cities? God considered this request, then agreed that if Abraham could find these righteous men in Sodom and Gomorrah, He would not destroy the cities. However, Abraham couldn't find these 50 men, so he went back to God and renegotiated, asking if He would be willing to accept 30 righteous men. God agreed, but again, Abraham was unable to find the men he was looking for.

This renegotiation went on, with God agreeing to spare the cities as long as Abraham would bring to him just ten righteous men. In the end, God spared the only righteous people in the city: Lot and his wife and daughters.

Now Abraham could have said to God, "*I* am a righteous man—will that be enough for you to spare these cities and their inhabitants?" Because Spirit is endlessly forgiving, we can negotiate with It again and again, yet we must also respect divine will because there's a sacred plan that we don't always know about.

We can't possibly see the whole picture as well as Spirit can. We might not realize that there is tremendous growth and learning in store for us if we actually take a course different from the comfortable one we would select from the level of serpent or jaguar. While we may long for material wealth and comfort, our soul was drawn to a family where we might have lacked these things. While we may have wanted loving and caring parents, we may have ended up with those who didn't give affection easily. Yet the perception from the level of hummingbird is that everything is perfect as it is, that nothing needs to be changed. From the level of eagle, we know that "the Father and I are One." There is no longer an "I," there is only Spirit, and there is no will other than that of Spirit. There is also no Doer other than God, and no effort required to accomplish anything. (This is the practice of nondoing, which we will discuss later.)

For luminous warriors, the real battle is to transcend the karmic lineage we've inherited. Then we can stop repeating the same mistakes that we made in the past and set us on a predetermined course in this life. The greatest challenge we face is inside us, and it is mythical. If we win the battle, we'll wake up from the nightmare of our personal and collective history, and *then* we can dream our existence into being.

In the same way that healing your past relationship wounds does not automatically bring you into a good relationship, healing your karmic lineage only makes you ready for the path—you then have to walk it. The way to do so is to practice the four practices: fearlessness, nondoing, certainty, and nonengagement.

The Practice of Fearlessness

To live fearlessly is to actively practice peace and non-violence, even when it seems like we're being threatened. This doesn't mean that we don't protect ourselves and our loved ones—it means that we don't respond from a place of anger or violence. Our propensity toward violent solutions is rooted in our brains, which are wired in a very strange way. The region where our sensations of pleasure are experienced is very close to the center where we experience violence, so when we stimulate one of these areas in the brain, we often end up stimulating the other.

We seem to be the only mammal whose brain is set up this way. This is why we (men in particular) so often associate violence with pleasure. We love a good action movie, especially the thrill of watching the good guy pump bullets into the bad guy. Most kids' computer games are all about blowing the enemy's brains out, and so-called erotic movies consist of acts of aggression committed against women every five minutes. And the sadomasochism we read about that is so common in wartime happens when these brain centers are overstimulated and develop four-lane highways between them. No wonder that, when faced with something that appears to be a problem, we enthusiastically don armor, unsheathe our sword, and declare war.

However, we do have other choices. The practices within each insight stimulate the brain centers associated with pleasure and bliss, thus deactivating the centers responsible for aggression. When we practice fearlessness, we can live in peace and practice nonviolence. When we embody peace, others in our presence feel a sense of calm and serenity. Even in times of war, we can live in an oasis of serenity.

The reason that fearlessness allows us to step beyond violence is because violence is rooted in fear—of being rejected, taken advantage of, ridiculed, hurt, and so on. Practicing fearlessness requires us to approach people and situations with love so that others can also let go of their apprehension and propensity toward violence.

In a world filled with rape, murder, and assault, this may seem like a timid response. When we wield a sword, we feel a sense of control and power. We revel in it, thriving on the aggressive, active role we're taking in changing the world, but we ignore the fact that violence only begets more violence. We think of war as a solution, but the violence we inflict on others makes them even more hostile. True, we may subdue them, but if we don't help them relinquish their anger or fear, all we've done is plant the seeds for the next skirmish.

We talk about a war on terror, a war on drugs, and a war on disease—it can be difficult to imagine how we might solve problems without declaring war on them, but we have to admit that these crusades only beget more terror, more drug use, and more disease. In the United States, the wealthiest country in the world, nearly 20 percent of our children go hungry every day, despite our so-called war on poverty. So how do we address these very real problems without resorting to a warlike response?

Fearlessness, Not War

Practicing fearlessness means that we first eliminate the poverty, terrorism, and war that rages inside of us. We eliminate our addiction to being right and fix *our perception* of every problem within us before we actually attempt the problem itself.

Many years ago, in their struggle to overcome their perceived scarcity, England and France attacked each other again and again. They cut down so many of their trees to build warships in order to battle each other for power and riches that, as a result, they deforested their countries, actually ending up with fewer resources for everyone. Had they recognized that they were the ones creating their feeling of scarcity, they could have found a more productive way to make sure that they had what they truly needed.

We, too, tend to overlook the price of waging a battle and instead focus on how we can get a bigger chunk of the pie. We don't like to think of ourselves as greedy—we're just cautious, building up a nest egg so that we will never feel insecure again. Of course we never reach this point because looking for security in marriage, the stock market, the workplace, real estate, or anything else material never quite manages to make us feel safe.

Luminous warriors build collaborative relationships with others instead of trying to conquer them; consequently, we get much closer to finding common ground and solutions to our mutual problems. Instead of clinging to our belief that we won't have enough or that we'll be taken advantage of, we bravely extend trust and find win-win solutions. This seems naive, of course, and part of us says that real life doesn't work this way. But the most successful organisms in nature are the result of collaborations. Even the human body is the product of a dozen organs and many different kinds of tissues working together.

We no longer have to buy into the false evidence that we have enemies we must continually battle and subdue. It's this mentality that leads us to get into shouting matches with the driver who takes "our" parking space, or to insist that our partner deliberately didn't unload the dishwasher in order to drive us crazy. Now we don't have to extend total trust to every person we come across or deny the danger of letting criminals run loose in the world—but we also don't have to walk through life with a sword drawn, ready to vanquish the accidentally inconsiderate.

As luminous warriors, we open our eyes so that we can see in others the capacity for peace, even if they aren't expressing it. Some psychologists would say that we project our dark side (our shadows) onto others, creating adversaries in order to avoid looking into our own unhealed selves. Yet making others wrong distracts us from the power we have to eliminate our own potential for being bullies and prevents us from accessing our creative, healing energy, which we can use to dream a better world.

When we practice fearlessness, we don't have to create enemies or obsess about "bad guys" in order to feel reassured that we're always righteous victims. It may seem strange that we would talk ourselves into feeling weak, but this works very well for us psychologically. If we see ourselves as victims, we excuse ourselves from any further sacrifices.

When we perceive at the level of serpent or jaguar instead of hummingbird, we focus on our adversaries and all their crimes against us, thus forgetting to ask the powerful question, *What's the opportunity for creating abundance and healing here?* At hummingbird, we try to find creative ways to negotiate with the people we disagree with, and we don't ignore our common ground because we become stuck in the belief that we're the good guys.

When we step beyond fear, violence, and death, we can embrace the way of the luminous warrior; we can wage peace, not war. Mahatma Gandhi is perhaps the finest example of a man who waged peace even in the face of violence, and he changed the course of history for one billion people. It cannot be so difficult to practice this for ourselves.

The Practice of Nondoing

We practice nondoing by immersing ourselves in the flow of the universe, receiving and working with the opportunities it presents to us rather than struggling to get everyone and everything to go along with our plans.

The luminous warrior's world isn't powered by aggression—her brilliance alone can vanquish the darkness. Nondoing means that rather than pushing and battling, we live in the light of love, creativity, and possibility; and we allow things to unfold as we surrender to the intelligence of the universe, trusting in its benevolence and abundance. When we practice nondoing, we don't put energy into doing things today that will take care of themselves by tomorrow. We don't micromanage our lives because we know in our very core that we're in the hands of Spirit.

In the West, we mistakenly believe that the only way to solve problems and get things done is to work hard. When we see someone who isn't being productive, we call him lazy. The Protestant ethic is about struggling because we've been ejected from the Garden of Eden and are destined to toil and sweat. We're taught that "idle hands do the work of the devil," so we don't trust ourselves with leisure time.

There's a story of a Mexican man who met a group of Australian Aborigines, and he asked if they had a notion of *mañana*. The man explained that to his people, *mañana* meant not rushing to do today what would take care of itself tomorrow.

The old people conferred among themselves, and after a good long while, one of them responded, "Yes, we do, but without such a sense of urgency about it."

The practice of nondoing doesn't require us to turn on, tune in, and drop out and spend our lives on top of a remote mountain. There are things we all need to do in order to survive and to keep our communities vibrant. But we don't have to take up residence in the "kingdom of do" and become possessed by our obligations (and our accomplishments). Even if we're occupied doing this or that, we don't have to identify with being busy and become addicted to activity. We can have an extremely long to-do list and still get everything important done by setting priorities and letting the little stuff go, confident that the universe will take care of the details. We can be fully present when at work, at rest, or with friends or family; and we can differentiate between the important, the trivial, and the insignificant. We can simply turn over to God what's crucial and forget about the rest.

We often get caught up in the hustle and bustle because we all love to feel our own importance. We convince ourselves that if we don't stay busy, something awful will happen. I'm always amused to watch people who are attending one of my lectures rush to the pay phones or pull out their cellular telephones as soon as there's a break. I would guess that maybe 5 percent of their calls are urgent—mostly they just like feeling that their office needs to hear from them or that there might be an important voice mail telling them that they need to do something.

Such busy-ness fosters the illusion that we'll live forever. With so much to do and so little time, we believe that we're so important that we can't possibly die. We tell ourselves that those who count on us can't possibly function if we don't do A, B, and C. Then when we're downsized or our child tells us he really doesn't need our help and asks us to leave him alone, we're utterly crushed. We hate being reminded that just like everyone else, we're expendable. Well, the world will continue to revolve around the sun, and humankind will continue to exist, even if we aren't around. Fearing this truth about ourselves, our ego convinces us to cling to self-importance.

Our constant bustle also makes it easier for us to avoid dealing with our emotions. When we pause and sense what we're feeling, we can be open to how the hand of Spirit might touch us in that very instant. Instead, we stunt our growth by avoiding those parts of ourselves that need healing, telling ourselves that we have too little time or not enough money to attend to the needs of our soul. We don't allow ourselves time in which to heal or dream.

Interestingly enough, when we stop thinking about what we "ought to" be doing and simply stay present to what *is* happening, we end up being far more productive and creative. We actually write that report instead of aimlessly surfing the Internet and then guiltily returning to the task at hand . . . which seems to be taking forever because we have trouble staying focused. Remaining in the moment instead of worrying about what has to get done this afternoon or next week opens our eyes to the possibilities we miss in all our rush to get things accomplished and prove how very important we are.

Try cultivating your own unimportance. The most successful, interesting people are the ones who don't take themselves seriously at all. They're amused by themselves, recognizing that life is an adventure with many unexpected twists and turns and cliff-hangers. Like good novelists, they go with the flow and see what unfolds as they creatively approach their lives, opening themselves up to opportunities. The stories they create are rich, surprising, and satisfying.

You practice nondoing by taking up residence in the level of eagle, where you cease to exist as separate from Spirit. Here there is no longer a doer; things simply happen.

The Practice of Certainty

To practice certainty is to have an unwavering commitment to the course you've chosen. That is, you let go of your worry that you're making a mistake or that you're not good enough, thin enough, rich enough, or young enough for an endeavor. For example, I know an entrepreneur who switched careers at the age of 70 and became a very successful painter. He never once doubted that he was an artist, even though everyone around him took his new direction with a smile and a grain of salt.

Certainty means that we deliberately choose not to leave ourselves any "escapes" that would allow us to keep one foot in the new track while keeping the other foot out the door. When we're in a relationship, for instance, we're not checking out other potential partners "just in case" there's someone better out there.

When I became a father for the first time in my late 30s, I was completely unprepared for the experience. In the back of my mind I told myself, "Well, if this parenting thing doesn't work out, I can always take my tent and return to the Amazon." After all, I had traveled to the Amazon many times and felt comfortable there. Parenting, an experience I'd never had before, was much more terrifying than the thought of being deep in the jungle and far from civilization.

The problem with my attitude was that it kept me from being fully present with my family, since deep in my heart I felt that I could up and leave at any point if things didn't work out. The minute you have a back door, you're blocked from creating what it is you want because your energies are divided. Failure becomes inevitable because you don't fully commit yourself. It's far better to burn your bridges behind you, lock all those back doors, and be completely engaged in the path you have chosen.

Of course you should be very informed about the decision you want to make and weigh the consequences carefully, but once you've made the choice, practice certainty. Thinking about whether your spouse is really the right one *after* you've already gotten married is not productive. And focusing on all the problems arising from your decision will block you from seeing the opportunities to create a great relationship.

So be courageous, but not foolish. Recognize if there are sharks in the water that you're going to swim in, and take the shark repellent with you. But once you've jumped in, don't start wondering what you're doing there . . . because then you'll become lunch.

The practice of certainty ensures that all your endeavors will have a positive outcome. Uncertainty, on the other hand, stems from fear, and will sabotage every move you make. So the first step in practicing certainty is to become familiar with your back doors. A student once told me that if things didn't work out for her to become a healer, she could always become a bag lady. While it comforted her to know that she could survive in the streets, I worked with her to shut this door because it was preselecting a future in which she would fail as a healer.

Back doors leak energy that could otherwise be available to fulfill your dreams. They are where fear lurks within you, and they lead to self-fulfilling prophecies of failure and defeat. However, there's a difference between a back door and an exit strategy. In other words, it's good to have an exit strategy in the event that the bicycle shop you and your friend are opening doesn't make it—then if things don't work out, you have a means to part ways amicably, without blaming the other for the business going under. Remember that certainty is driven by love and fearlessness, but a back door is driven by fear. Burn your bridges behind you so that you have no option but success.

The Practice of Nonengagement

When you practice nonengagement, you deliberately choose not to take part in battles, particularly those where the grounds of engagement are defined by your adversary. Just because someone is itching for a fight, longing to create a drama that will allow them to feel like a noble rescuer or a victim, that doesn't mean you have to play along. And the people you're closest to are experts at pushing all of your buttons. Your spouse and your children know how to bring you to the edge of insanity and fierce skirmishes in seconds.

I remember asking a friend of mine who was a fighter pilot what the military taught him about aerial dogfights, like the ones that I'd seen on television as a child. He explained to me that you never engage in a fight in the sky if you can possibly help it—you want the fight to be over before your adversary even knows you were there. The goal is to conserve your energy and use it the way you want to, instead of wearing yourself out engaging in a confrontation that someone else is intent on having. The minute you engage, he explained, you've already lost.

So if you choose to enter an argument, be aware that you're doing it for sport, sparring because you enjoy it, not because it will allow you to vanquish your adversary of the moment or will prove you right. The Earthkeepers say that if you battle the conquistador, you'll never win; in fact, the best you can hope for is a stalemate. You come back to your tent bloodied, sharpen your sword, and return the next day to an utterly fruitless battle. The question is: Do you want to prove yourself "right," or do you want to connect with your opponent and find common ground and win? Do you want to perpetuate and maintain your point of view, or do you want to solve a problem?

We rarely ask ourselves these questions because we're unconsciously drawn to battles that are choreographed by the stories we've written about our lives. If our story is one of being underappreciated and misunderstood, then our ego is continually on the lookout for chances to prove that this is the case. If we're in line at the store and someone cuts in front of us, we jump at the opportunity to confront them and demand the respect we're due. Should those we care about forget to do something we asked them to do, we insist that their motive was pure selfishness and confront them about their lack of respect for us. Meanwhile, the real story might be that the other person was simply distracted or preoccupied with his own troubles and would actually feel bad and apologize if we said, "When you blocked my car in the driveway, it was really inconvenient for me." Rather than give him a chance to explain himself, we choose to perpetuate our story.

Of course we sometimes find ourselves in situations where people are totally committed to creating a drama and playing a particular role. In such cases, it's very difficult not to give in to the temptation of playing our part in the battle they've planned. But if we make a point of being luminous warriors and fighting our true adversary (our wounded self) instead of projecting it out into the world, it will be easier to disengage. If I'm angry with my partner because she doesn't agree with me, I know that it's better to resolve the conflict within myself rather than to pick a fight with her, hoping to bring her around to my position. I will sometimes say to my partner, "This sounds like an invitation for me to defend myself," and avoid an argument. Engaging in a crusade because I'm unhealed simply perpetuates my own victim/bully/rescuer drama.

What We're Willing to Give Up

To practice nonengagement, we have to be totally negotiable yet completely uncompromising. This means that we have to be willing to negotiate, which means giving something up. We may have to give up our desire to be seen as superior or our need to micromanage every detail of a situation. We may have to give up our rigid notions about how something should be done. In Jonathan Swift's *Gulliver's Travels,* two nations go to war over a disagreement about whether soft-boiled eggs should be eaten from the large end or the small end. It's an absurd image, but we often become intractable about our position rather than focusing on the importance of resolving the issues. We get into quagmires, unable to move forward because we're so attached to our stories that we can't identify anything we're willing to surrender.

Our unwillingness to be flexible can be seen not only in our personal lives, but also in international relations. The second round of Strategic Arms Limitations Talks (SALT II) lead to a treaty between the United States and the Soviet Union back in 1979, but the U.S. never ratified it because they couldn't agree with the Soviets on the number of inspections of Soviet nuclear sites the Americans would be allowed to make and vice versa. No one talked about how those inspections might be conducted or what an inspection entailed. Would the Russians go through top secret files at our nuclear installations? Would they only stop by for tea? These details were never discussed.

Instead, the talks became deadlocked on the *number* of inspections each side would be allowed every year. Negotiators on both sides became increasingly suspicious of each other and more entrenched in their own positions: For example, the Soviets wanted only five inspections per year, while the Americans required seven. Neither country had to agree to a lack of any accountability from the other, yet both sides refused to be more creative in negotiating common ground.

Even as we strive to come to agreements with others, when we practice nonengagement, we have to be completely uncompromising when it comes to our integrity or the things we deeply believe in. To do so, we have to be very clear about what our real values are, so we can negotiate efficiently rather than exhausting ourselves by becoming trapped in an endless war over insignificant details.

As luminous warriors, we step beyond fear and death and are able to bring love and beauty to every encounter. Now we are ready to walk the way of the seer.

INSIGHT 3

The Way of the Seer

———————————————■———————————————

To be a seer is to walk softly on the earth and dream destiny.

In this modern world, the dreamtime has been consigned to the domain of sleep. To experience it, you have to lie down, close your eyes, and enter that deep reverie where images appear to you. Yet for an Earthkeeper, there's little difference between the sleeping and the waking dreams of everyday life, with all of their mystery and drama. Earthkeepers try to be fully awake even while asleep, in contrast to ordinary people who are fully asleep even while awake. When awake, Earthkeepers are able to dream a world of grace and beauty into being. In this chapter, *you* will learn how to create with your eyes wide open, and you'll understand why your dreams (and nightmares) always come true.

The word *dream* often has a negative connotation for us because we think that it's a waste of time when done in the day and meaningless at night, or at best a message from our subconscious to be decoded in the morning. We don't realize that we actually generate the reality we live in, that we dream the world into being—so our ability to craft beautiful visions while awake is very important.

When you master the art of dreaming with your eyes open, you can stop going through life unconsciously. You can begin to create a rich life instead of settling for the collective nightmare thought up for you by society—then you are the author of the epic poem of your life, rather than an unwitting participant in the events occurring around you. When you learn to dream, you no longer have to act out scripts that cast you as the victim, the rescuer, or the perpetrator. You can free yourself from the limitations of your stories, instead of clinging to them in order to give yourself a false sense of security.

The hummingbird's quality of stillness in flight is required here. You must go beyond inspirational words or just thinking about how to solve problems and enter into the stillness of your soul, crafting a vision of what you want your world to be—whether it's an image of your own life or of that of everyone on the planet.

Becoming Aware of Your Waking Dreams

To begin crafting your vision, you must become aware of your waking dreams and their symbolism. In psychoanalysis, you learn that every symbol in your nighttime images represents a part of you: The scary ghost, the fair damsel, and the burning house can all be interpreted as aspects of your self. For example, when I was in graduate school I once dreamed that I was inside a tunnel and there was a locomotive speeding toward me, its single lamp glaring menacingly as it rushed at me. I went to one of my professors, who was very skilled at dream analysis, and related my nightmare. I assumed that I was myself in the dream and that the locomotive represented my course load at the university, which I felt was overwhelming me, threatening to squash me before I could manage to graduate.

My professor agreed that this could be the case, but it was only the superficial interpretation of my dream. He then asked me what part of me was the locomotive that was rushing headlong out of control, unaware of what was on its path. Then he asked what part of me was the tunnel that held all of these aspects safely within it. I recognized that part of myself felt overwhelmed, but that I also felt a tremendous sense of purpose and direction represented by the locomotive, and that all of these elements were held in the safety of the tunnel inside the earth, which was my subconscious.

You can apply the same analytical approach to examining your waking dreams. Symbols are everywhere, and everything that you experience mirrors a part of you—so when you can perceive reality in this way, you understand how you're already dreaming your world.

Once I visited a medicine woman in the American Southwest. She lived in a wooden shack above the tree line and had a reputation as one who could help you understand the hidden messages in your dreams. The trail to her home wasn't well marked, and several times I had to backtrack and try a different path. Toward the end, I became lost and had to scamper up a steep embankment to the top of a ravine. During my climb, I slipped and twisted my ankle, so I had to hobble the rest of the way to her hut. By that time I was angry and covered in sweat, wondering what made me attempt this journey in the first place.

I greeted the old woman, who summarily asked me what I wanted so far away from civilization. I explained that I had been nearby visiting a renowned medicine man and had heard about her skill at interpreting dreams. I wanted her help in understanding a very unsettling dream I'd had a few nights earlier. She looked at me warily, yet after a few moments she invited me to sit down, remarking, "First, let's interpret your morning. Tell me how it was getting here, and I will tell you about yourself."

As I looked out the window, I saw her pickup truck parked in the driveway . . . and a clean, gravel road leading up to her cottage. It turns out that I had picked the most difficult way to get to her. I then understood how my journey to her home was symbolic of how I tromped through life: I would often take the wrong path, become frustrated, lose my patience, and end up in a desperate situation where I had to scale up the most difficult way, and I'd hurt myself in the process. This was exactly how I'd gone through graduate school and the early years of my research in the Amazon, where I earned a reputation among fellow anthropologists for being able to get lost in the most unlikely places. In my eagerness to understand the mysterious symbols in my nighttime dream, I'd been completely overlooking the meaning of the events in my daytime reverie.

American Dreams

When we sleep, we usually feel that we have little or no control over what unfolds in our awareness—and we often feel the same way when we're awake. We're continually told that events "happen" to us, that the best we can do to change our world is to work harder and try to influence other people into acting the way we'd like them to. We make rules and try to strictly enforce them, but it's never enough. (It's interesting to note that five of the Ten Commandments aim to regulate the impulses of our primitive reptilian and mammalian brains, which are associated with the levels of serpent and jaguar.) We don't consider that we might envision things differently and come up with far more creative approaches to solving our dilemmas. This process requires us to shift into the level of hummingbird from that of serpent and jaguar, which are primitive and self-absorbed states. At such lower levels of perception, we remain engrossed in the cultural trance that we've been educated into.

In the United States, there's now a news channel that strives not to widen people's perspectives but to reflect back to them what they already believe. Its viewers seek comfort in the reassurance that the world is an untrustworthy place, filled with good people like them who are responsible neighbors and share their beliefs, and bad people who do terrible things and think differently.

As a result of being caught up in our cultural trance, we in America no longer live in a democracy; we live in a "mediacracy." The media is so heavily influenced by its corporate sponsors that even the world's events are editorialized into opinion pieces. As far back as 1880, John Swinton, a writer at *The New York Times,* was quoted as saying, "The business of journalists is to destroy the truth. . . . We are the tools and vassals of rich men behind the scenes." This sentiment continues today: Because advertisers who finance the news are interested in creating good consumers who buy their burgers, they have no interest in helping us look or think outside the box.

When we simply gulp down any- and everything that's served to us on the morning news, we lose our creativity and the ability to make our planet what we want it to be. While we can't dream up a world in which there's no crime, we *can* envision one in which crime and violence have no place in our lives—where we are neither the victims nor the perpetrators of such acts.

Our Power to Create a Better Life

Let's get right down to it: Reality isn't so hot for most of us. If it were, there would be fewer of us taking drugs or drinking alcohol to escape our misery. For most people, reality is a nightmare, not a pleasant dream.

Now, it's very politically charged to say that all individuals have the ability to create or change their reality. Are the 300 million living in poverty in India simply not doing the right kind of dreaming? What about those who were killed in the tsunami that hit Southeast Asia in 2004 or left homeless by Hurricane Katrina the following year in the U.S.? In the face of such human misery, it's easy to dismiss the notion that we dream our world into being as New Age fluff. It may seem more sensible to blame such catastrophes on the forces of poverty, which put people in harm's way. Many think that if we eliminated poverty, there would be no suffering—but wealth does not cure misery. Some of the unhappiest individuals I have ever met live in the lap of luxury, while many of the happiest I've been with count few material comforts.

The notion that we dream our world into being mustn't be used as an apology for staying uninvolved socially or avoiding those in need. Rather, such tragedies need to move us to do even more to assist others so that we don't wait for large-scale disasters to wake us up to the need to share our resources and stop the destruction of the environment. And we can dream a world in which these tragedies don't happen to us.

If many of us hold a dream of hope and possibility, we can make a huge difference. One of the reasons I publish my books with Hay House, for instance, is that they're committed to changing the world for the better. My accountant was baffled when I turned down a big New York publisher who offered me more money to publish my books with them. But Hay House donates all profits from their South African book sales to children with AIDS who have been left parentless, and I love that my books are helping to support these efforts. What's more, I know that I'm part of a team—from those in shipping and receiving to the salespeople—that shares a common vision of the kind of world we could dream together.

As a seer, you can choose to reject the nightmare that's presented to you by the media and the people around you. You don't have to participate in the dream that says that the purpose of everyone's life is to be a completely obedient child and excellent student and then graduate to marriage, family, a steady job, a house in a nice neighborhood, and a television with 200 channels . . . after which you retire to a comfortable gated community. While this may be the American dream, it doesn't have to be yours. (It's certainly not mine!) There are so many more interesting dreams you can create.

Too often we take for granted what our collective dream tells us is possible or impossible, acceptable or unacceptable. Recently, someone I know moved from New York City to a smaller metropolitan area. Despite the many bus routes, bike trails, and transport services in her new city, along with her proximity to a business district, many of her new neighbors were shocked by her decision not to buy a car. They insisted that she couldn't possibly bear the inconvenience of walking several blocks to the grocery store in cold weather, even though she'd done just that for years when she was living in Manhattan. Because these individuals were so used to hopping into their cars to do chores, they perceived my friend's decision as radical. They weren't used to dreaming outside the box and being open to new possibilities.

In fact, most of us are unaware that we're being dreamed and that we might envision something else that's uniquely ours. We only recognize this when we escape from our very limited experience and are exposed to something new—for example, when a young person from the Bible Belt goes off to college, the Army, or the big city, and he or she is shocked to find that there are people who are agnostic and yet very decent and ethical.

I had an experience in my early days while training with my Laika mentor that showed me the limitations of my beliefs. Don Antonio and I were walking on the Altiplano—an arid, mountainous plateau that stretches from Cusco to Lake Titicaca in Peru—and I explained that the Christian tradition instructs us to turn to heaven whenever we need help or guidance. He smiled and said that the Laika ask our Mother Earth for help, not the heavens.

I was obstinately holding on to my position that the divine was above when we entered a small village, immediately spying three horses to our right. Don Antonio pointed to the fresh horse manure and asked me to bring a scoop over to where we were. I found a piece of cardboard to use as a shovel, and when I returned to where he stood, I saw that he had dug a shallow hole in the earth. "Put half of it in here," he said. I did so, and he covered it up with soil. Then he pointed to a large boulder nearby and asked me to place the rest of the manure on top of the rock. We then walked away, and he refused to say another word about the subject.

Two weeks later we came back to the same village. By now I'd forgotten the conversation and my mentor's mysterious instructions about the horse manure . . . but he hadn't. Don Antonio walked straight to where the hole had been and said, "Dig." When I'd gone a few inches below the surface, he said, "See? It's already turning back into fertilizer." He then walked me over to the boulder and pointed to the dry dung, explaining, "See? It still looks like shit, doesn't it? Still smells like shit, no? Our Mother mulches everything back into life: all of our pain, our sorrow, our grief, even our waste."

All my life, I had believed that the divine resides above us. Even the Lord's Prayer says, "Our Father, Who art in heaven . . ." I wasn't ready to entertain the notion that the divine is dark, rich, and moist—like the feminine earth—or that the sacred is present in our everyday life, in the ground we walk upon, not in some pure, clean, celestial dwelling, far removed from all our "crap."

Even though as an anthropologist I'd been trained to respect other people's beliefs, I still held my own to be superior to those of the primitive peoples I was studying—after all, *I* had a Ph.D. I didn't even know that I was trapped in the dream that had been envisioned for me by my culture, religion, and education. I learned then that the collective dream most of us are living is the garish fairy tale we confuse for reality. It's invisible to us because we're not conscious of the fact that it is merely a dream.

The other lesson I learned that day was that what I'd perceived as filthy excrement was actually on its way to becoming fertilizer and food for other life. In psychology, I'd been trained to put the shit up on the stone, dissect it, examine it under the microscope to determine its origin and composition, and then ponder how such fine food could have turned into this.

It's the same way that we wonder, *How could such a promising relationship have turned into crap?* Well, once we start perceiving things from a higher perspective, we can see beyond problems to opportunities and potential for growth. As don Antonio used to tell me, "Alberto, you're a weeder. You're constantly pulling up the weeds in your life—the childhood traumas and your early lost loves. Your garden is weed free, but you've planted no flowers or fruits. Let yourself have some weeds so that you can cultivate things of beauty."

My training as a psychologist had me wrapped up in the belief that life is full of problems, and if I just worked hard enough I could come up with all the solutions. I wasn't dreaming a peaceful, fruitful existence, but a problem-ridden one, and that's what the universe provided to me.

How We Dream the World into Being

What we see and experience is the world we're dreaming into being—if we don't like it, we can open our eyes, be conscious, and create something different. One way to do so is through prayer, which can have a powerful effect on certain situations. One of my favorite examples comes from a study of 400 patients in the coronary care unit at San Francisco General Hospital in the 1980s. Researcher

Randolph Byrd set up an experiment in which half of the patients were prayed for, in addition to receiving the routine medical care that all patients received. The doctors and nurses didn't know which of the patients were being prayed for. While none of those who were prayed for experienced cardiac arrest or died, 12 of those in the control group suffered cardiac arrest, and 3 died.

We're used to praying by making specific requests of the divine, but it's more powerful to allow Spirit to take care of the outcome of any situation. Researchers for an organization called the Spindrift Foundation have studied the power of prayer to heal simple organisms, such as sprouting seeds. (When noting the effects of prayer, plants are easy to work with—after all, they don't exercise, eat differently, take vitamin supplements, or have people outside of the study praying for them.) Two types were tested: (1) *directed prayer,* in which the supplicant tells the divine what the problem is and what outcome he desires, such as having his aunt fully recover from a stroke; and (2) *nondirected prayer,* in which the person praying tells the divine the name of the recipient but doesn't seek a specific outcome, requesting only that "Thy will be done." The Spindrift Foundation plant studies showed that both strategies work, but that nondirected prayer is four times as effective as directed prayer because we don't need to tell Spirit what to do.

As a form of prayer, visualization works at the level of hummingbird, using the language of images. We may form a clear picture of living in a big house on the ocean, for instance. As I explained earlier, visualization is much more powerful than affirmations, which work at the level of the mind (jaguar) and employ the language of words. We know that a picture is worth a thousand words, so to truly create world peace, we need to pray a peaceful world

133

into being from the level of hummingbird. Otherwise, how can a single visualization of world peace counteract the 100 images of war and terror we see in an average 30-minute news program?

The Reality We Create

The universe always mirrors back to us the conditions of our dreaming. So if we're fearful that money won't come to us, it won't. However, if we experience abundance with what we have today, even if we don't actually have money right now, we will have abundance, and we can be sure that further riches are on their way to us.

So when our life isn't working for us, the most effective solution isn't to change our career, spouse, exercise routine, or community, but to work on the purity of our dreaming. We change our dream and our relationship or career comes into balance. This doesn't mean that we remain in an abusive relationship or terrible job, but it does mean that we don't leave the relationship or job wounded, blaming it for victimizing us. We rid ourselves of the unproductive stories and envision the experiences we'd like to have instead.

There's an old story about a traveler who meets another voyager on the road coming from the other direction. The first man says, "I'm headed for the town you just came from. Tell me, what's it like? Are the people good, honest, and trustworthy?" The second traveler says, "Well, what was everyone like in the town you just left?" The first traveler says, "Oh, they were terrible! I was robbed, denied lodgings, and overcharged for food. There isn't a decent person in that town." The second traveler says, "Well, then, that's exactly what you'll find in the town you're headed toward."

What the second traveler recognizes, which the first traveler does not, is that wherever you go, there you are. You bring the energy of your beliefs, your mental state, and your emotions into every circumstance, and the universe responds by meeting your expectations. There is no objective reality, because your prophecies are all self-fulfilling. This is dreaming.

We can achieve anything we want by truly believing in the dream we'd like to experience and following the way of the seer. We do this through the practices of beginner's mind, living consequently, transparency, and integrity.

The Practice of Beginner's Mind

Practicing beginner's mind requires us to let go of our preconceived notions. As Jesus said, "Except ye . . . become as little children, ye shall not enter into the kingdom of heaven." In other words, our lives become much simpler when we aren't weighed down by the baggage of our stories and expectations. The Laika say that this is when we are able to walk in the snow without leaving tracks. We stop being jaded, and instead open ourselves up to the opportunities presented to us. Innocence and spontaneity infuse our lives again, and we lose the attitude of "been there, done that." We become childlike, experiencing things as if for the first time.

Zen practitioners strive to achieve what's known as "empty mind." There's a story about a master and his student, who's becoming quite impressed with himself and all that he's learned. The teacher invites his student to tea and fills his cup until it begins to overflow. Shocked, the student cries out, "But master, the cup is already full!" To which the teacher replies, "How can I teach you if your mind is also too full?"

Contrast this to the West, where the more you know with your "full" mind, the more you're worth. The practice of beginner's mind requires us to let go of this belief and become amateurs. In fact, the word *amateur* comes from a French word meaning "lover." Amateurs are lovers of life, enthralled by how different each day and experience is. To be amateurs, we have to let go of our expertise. Yet understand that when we practice beginner's mind, we don't *forget* about our years of experience—we simply don't confuse what we learned yesterday with what we're discovering today.

We have to say to ourselves, "This is what I believe might be true, but let me test it out against reality." We develop a hypothetical relationship with life instead of a fixed one. Then if we encounter a situation we've been in before, we don't assume the outcome, because when we do, it becomes a self-fulfilling prophecy. We say, "This looks like an argument with my spouse. In fact, it seems to be the same one about money that we get into all the time. But maybe it isn't—maybe it's something else."

Suddenly, we find that we're not in a marital spat; rather, we're being presented with the chance to see a situation from our spouse's point of view. Instead of hearing, "You should go back to that job you hate because you're not carrying your half of the load," we hear, "I'm scared." We notice this as an opportunity to offer our support and find a way to reconnect in a loving way, further cementing our relationship.

Recently, I was pulled over by a police officer for speeding. I immediately became angry at myself for being so stupid as to drive 70 miles per hour (mph) in a 50 mph zone, then I was resentful that I was caught . . . and then I decided to practice beginner's mind. When the officer reached my car, I opened my window, smiled, and said, "I know that I was speeding, and I deserve to get a ticket. I don't have an excuse. How's your day going?" He ended up talking to me about his struggle with chronic fatigue, didn't give me a ticket, and was delighted when I offered him a copy of my book *Shaman, Healer, Sage.* For this to work, of course, it had to be authentic, without any ulterior motive of getting out of a ticket. And it did work—both the officer and I had a new experience.

Letting Go of What You Know

Practicing beginner's mind has a lot in common with scientific theory. In science, we form a hypothesis based on what we've observed, and then we test it against the facts. If the evidence doesn't fit the theory, we throw out the hypothesis. This is very different from religion, in which the hypothesis is considered holy. In religion, we test out our hypothesis against the facts, and if the facts don't fit, we keep the theory and throw out any contradictory evidence. This is why overwhelming scientific data of human evolution over millions of years doesn't change the thinking of a fundamentalist who believes that God created the world in six days, and that all the dinosaurs lived in harmony with Adam and Eve in the Garden of Eden. (A recent Gallup Poll indicates that close to 47 percent of the population in the United States believes that God created human beings pretty much in their present form at one time within the last 10,000 years.)

Practicing beginner's mind requires us to give up our dogma, whatever it is. Of course this is easier said than done when that dogma seems to have served us well. I remember trying to explain to my grandmother about the virgin birth of Christ. She had no reason to give up her life-long belief that the mother of Jesus was literally a virgin, so my argument that this description was meant to be taken figuratively—that Jesus was born of a mother who was pure in heart and uncorrupted—didn't sway her in the least. *All* dogma is dangerous. While my grandmother's beliefs may seem benign on the surface, countless people have gone to war to protect this and similar beliefs.

And while we think of religion as being rigid, science can become rigidly ideological as well, as if it were a body of knowledge instead of *a way of acquiring* knowledge. In the early days of my research, for instance, I found that many scientists rejected out of hand the research that I was doing because it didn't fit into the assumptions they held. Then as quantum physics and chaos theory became more popularly accepted, my work became increasingly recognized by scientists and physicians. The dogma of science is that we often resist asking bigger questions that might result in enormous strides in our ability to heal ourselves and the planet.

While we expect children to say unusual and illogical things, and we're amused by their creative questions and ideas, adults who break away from ideology and wonder about possibilities are often written off as lunatics or considered half crazy. In 1899, the Serbian inventor Nikola Tesla claimed that while he was working in his Colorado Springs laboratory, he received energy signals from Mars in the form of clicks. Tesla was much ridiculed, but about a hundred years later, researchers discovered that he hadn't been imagining things: They realized that he'd probably picked up on natural radio waves that are commonly transmitted by gas clouds and other cosmic materials. Tesla was a visionary whose technological inventions include alternating current; wireless telegraphy; the power plant at Niagara Falls; and, most famously, the Tesla coil used in radios (which generates high voltage). All of these must have seemed completely preposterous when he first spoke about them.

There's great danger in collapsing truths into beliefs that limit us, because we'll always be taken by surprise in the future. We know that the cutting edge of medical treatment 20 years ago is outdated today, for instance, and that the discoveries of avant-garde physicists that were accepted by the previous generation have been proven erroneous.

Our challenge is to move beyond our sense that there's only what is true and what is not true, and that there's only real and unreal, with nothing in between. In the same way that when we were children we believed that communicating long distances through the air, walking on the moon, or cloning were "impossible"—strict beliefs about what can and can't be done prevent us from dreaming the world we desire.

Achieving Beginner's Mind

We can return to a more creative, open, childlike way of being by making simple changes in our routines and habits, such as eating with the opposite hand, taking a different route home, and smiling instead of fuming when we're upset. We can shatter our complicity with the mediocrity around us and open ourselves up to a much wider range of possibilities.

Now it's important not to get stuck in the literal interpretation of this practice. There was a CEO of a major corporation who was told by a consultant that he would become more creative if he took his shoes off while attending business meetings. It may have made some difference in his ability to break out of his usual way of thinking, but this gesture on its own wasn't enough to make a difference in how he ran his business. He thought he'd found a magic bullet, a shortcut to creativity, but he was only breaking out of the confines of his shoes on the most literal level. He needed to let go of the beliefs that were holding him in place—in other words, the *soul* he needed to set free was not the *sole* of his foot.

The following exercise will help you open yourself up to the new by getting rid of what's not working for you.

EXERCISE: Clear the Junk Out of Your Life

To practice beginner's mind, you must clear the debris out of your life. At the level of serpent, this means emptying your closets of all the junk and "collectibles" you know you don't need but have been reluctant to get rid of. (After you die, your children will throw it all away anyway.) This clutter keeps you tied to the past—that stuffed animal you won at the county fair, that college sweatshirt you've outgrown and have no occasion to wear anyway, and so on. You'll still remember the pleasures of those experiences, but without the tangible symbols that are stuffing your closets.

Throw away that lava lamp you never liked, which represents the lifestyle you thought you were supposed to have back in your bachelor years. Let go of the books you feel you really ought to read someday and the craft projects you feel compelled to complete even though you've lost interest in them. Allow yourself to release the expectations you had of yourself, and accept that you've made different choices.

Clear out your attic, your basement, and your over-loaded bookshelves and CD racks. Let go of the belief that you have to continue to possess any object that might be "worth something." Give it to the less fortunate, rather than clinging to the illusion that the more objects you possess, the more security and prosperity you have.

Make your home, desk, car, closet, and *mind* minimalist spaces.

◇

At the level of jaguar, we practice beginner's mind by chucking limiting beliefs about scarcity, abundance, inti-macy, and self-worth. Ultimately, we realize that *every* belief is limiting, and we toss them all into the recycling bin. We then develop a hypothetical relationship with the world, testing every notion we have for its usefulness. We under-stand that "believing is seeing," and that the universe will validate every belief we hold about the nature of reality.

At the level of the sacred, beginner's mind means not identifying with our thoughts. From the perspective of hummingbird, we understand that every thought is an affirmation that reinforces an unconscious mental model about the nature of reality. When we stop identifying with our thoughts, the ego dissolves, because it stems from the belief that *I think, therefore I am*. We need to take every single belief we have about the nature of our reality and fling it in the fire. After they've been incinerated, we're free to reinvent ourselves and our world. And then, from the perspective of eagle, the amateur within us finds the true beloved—Spirit.

The Practice of Living Consequently

The second practice in the way of the seer entails that you recognize the impact each action you take has on future generations. Many Native Americans believe that their every act affects the destiny of seven generations into the future; Earthkeepers understand that even thoughts have an impact on tomorrow, so they're mindful of every image and feeling they experience.

The exception is when you act from the level of eagle. Here there are no ulterior motives for your actions, since there are no thoughts or images. You don't seek personal gain; rather, you use your personal power for the good of all. When you do so, your actions don't disturb the ripples of tomorrow because you're in perfect harmony with the matrix of creation. Your actions are like burnt seeds that no longer bear any fruit, and you aren't accruing karma— you're in perfect ayni.

On a practical level, as Earthkeepers we don't become so self-involved that we leave a trail of destruction behind us as we noisily tromp a path in the woods. When we're aware of the effects of our actions seven generations down the road, we don't try to calculate just how much pollution we can dump into the environment and still protect our profit margin; instead, we recognize the true cost of poisoning our resources. We're aware that our children's children will be drinking the same water and breathing the same air that we are.

I clearly remember one summer when I was a teenager. I was riding in a car with four of my friends, and I pulled a carton of milk out of our cooler. I was about to take a swig when I realized that it had turned sour; in disgust, I threw it out the window. Immediately, I saw the carton lying in naked contrast to the beautiful green forest alongside the road, and its ugliness made a powerful impression on me. Now whenever I'm hiking, I pick up any garbage I see. It's so easy to do, and I know that by removing the litter, I'm beautifying the forest, not only for myself and for others who might come along, but for generations to come.

Living consequently means that without having to agonize over it, you sell the SUV and choose to limit your burning of fossil fuels because you know that such a vehicle's exhaust will cut a larger hole in the ozone layer. It means that when you purchase something, you recognize that you're supporting that store or company and its policies, so you spend a little more money to buy the item from one whose ethics you subscribe to, one who respects the environment and compensates its workers well.

When you practice living consequently, you're fully conscious of the impact of each thought, intention, and action you have, and you take care to make them positive and healing instead of selfish and destructive. You recognize when you're acting out of fear, and you deliberately choose to act out of love instead. You take full responsibility for all your actions, and the universe notices this, making your good (as well as your bad) karma immediate. Since you get instant feedback and support for all of your actions, you won't leave the grocery store when the clerk has given you too much change—you'll feel compelled to return it. Then you'll get the reward back tenfold.

Emotional and Generational Curses

In this practice, we also become aware of the consequences of our behavior. The emotional wounds we cause to others can be so powerful that they can be felt not only over a lifetime, but for generations. In the Amazon, they refer to these as *generational curses:* The terror that a troubled mother inflicts on her daughters is felt by their daughters and their daughters' daughters, and the harsh punishment a father exacts on his son is felt by many generations. This operates on a collective level as well. For example, the legacy of colonialism and slavery didn't disappear when the original slaves died—their experiences affected the way they raised their children and the way those children raised *their* children. This is also true in families where there's alcoholism, mental illness, or abuse. Even the grandkids of people who lost everything during the Great Depression still deal with issues of scarcity.

Generational curses are often invisible to us, since we're born with them and consider them part of our "skin." It's important to be aware of such legacies so that we can heal them instead of damning our children to living in reaction to a wound that was inflicted on our grandmother 75 years ago. Living consequently means healing this wound rather than passing it on as an inheritance to our children.

When you believe that someone you're close to is caught in the grip of a story that is not her own, you can offer wisdom, guidance, and support. But please keep in mind that if you become self-righteous and play the role of noble rescuer, you cast her in the role of hapless victim who needs some "tough love," and you start to impose your dogma on her. There's nothing more frustrating than hearing someone smugly say, "Drop your story already and get over it."

The Practice of Transparency

You practice transparency when you stop hiding the parts of yourself that make you uncomfortable.

Once when I was getting on a bus in the Inka highlands with don Antonio, he chose to become invisible to everyone but me. I could see him, but I soon realized that no one else could. We had several buses to take on our journey, and to my amazement, every time we lined up and boarded, the bus drivers asked for the tickets of every traveler except my mentor—it was as if they looked right through him. At one point, a heavyset woman carrying a small child and a chicken came on board, and I wouldn't have been surprised if she'd sat down on don Antonio's lap, unable to see that he was right there next to me.

When *we* practice transparency, however, we don't have to do it literally. It simply means that we allow others to see us and that we have nothing to hide. After all, it's what we're trying to conceal that's actually the most visible to other people. When we see an arrogant man bossing someone around or bragging about himself, we clearly see that underneath all that bluster, he's insecure about his power and importance. When we see a lovely young woman dressed in baggy clothing with her hair hiding her face, we know that she's feeling unattractive and fearful of rejection.

But we hide more than our insecurities. Oftentimes we hide our beauty and power as well because we're uncomfortable with them or fear the consequences of letting our light shine. One of my students, for instance, was a very smart young woman who was married to an older man. She continually masked her intelligence because her husband found it threatening. After completing her training, she realized that she could no longer pretend to be a trophy wife—so she persuaded her spouse to join her book club and engage in activities with her that she found intellectually stimulating.

Practicing transparency doesn't mean that you have to become a target. If you've chosen to walk a spiritual path, you don't have to hide it for fear of ridicule. Another of my students is a nurse and felt the need to conceal the fact that she was a healer and practiced energy medicine with her hospital patients (as well as performing her conventional medical duties, of course). She was afraid that at any time she might be discovered and fired, and perhaps lose her license. But as her patients kept getting better and doctors continued to try to place their patients on her floor, she realized that she was trying to hide her greatest asset. She didn't need to explain to anyone what she did or believed in—she only had to reveal herself, at the level of the sacred, which is beyond words and explanation, and acknowledge what others could already see.

When we have nothing left to hide, we become transparent. In my previous books, which were quite autobiographical, I revealed a lot about myself. People asked me if I was concerned that strangers as well as friends now knew so much about me, and I explained that I was actually happy that I now had nothing left to conceal. All of my failings and foibles were out there in the open, and I didn't have to expend energy to cover them up.

Hiding our true selves attract to us those who embody that which we keep secret. It externalizes our healing process, entangling us in another person's drama and leaving us more vulnerable and fragile than we were before. It also causes us to become identified with a story, such as "I'm easily taken advantage of, so I need to act tough and abrasive in this negotiation," or "I'm easily hurt, so I'd better not attract a lover." We bury the unhealed part of ourselves deep inside, and the wound remains there until someone comes along to rub a little salt on it to remind us of our need for growth.

When we practice full disclosure about who we are and stop trying to hide parts of ourselves in order to please others, fit in, or prevent ourselves from experiencing pain, other people can become confused because they, too, have bought into our old story. It's okay if those around us don't understand or embrace our many facets—it's human nature to try to categorize and pigeonhole each other, even though we're all a bundle of contradictions. So at the level of serpent, I tell people that I'm an anthropologist. In jaguar, I let them know that I study how we make ourselves ill and how we can make ourselves well, and that I also train Western shamans. In hummingbird, I look into their eyes and say nothing because words cannot describe my being. In eagle, I invite them to taste the One Spirit that we share.

Most strangers I sit next to on airplanes are content to learn that I'm a teacher or anthropologist. They have a way to tag me, and then we can go on to talk about the weather. I don't need to explain to them that there are realms beyond what we can see or hear. But I don't hide who I am—if I meet someone who's truly curious and I believe it can make a difference, I talk to him or her on a spiritual level and we discuss things of real substance.

Transparency means establishing congruence between who you say you are and who you really are. It means "walking your talk." But you can't show your true self to others when you don't know who you are. In an earlier exercise, you learned that you're not your roles: You're not mother, executive, son, or daughter, but these are parts that you play, and you can't be contained by such limited definitions. The real you is the seer, who observes all you do yet is unaffected by any of your thoughts or actions. This is the one who can't be defined by any role, age, or social standing.

The Practice of Integrity

You practice integrity by being true to your word and recognizing its power to create reality. After all, in the Bible, it's said that "in the beginning was the Word . . . and the Word was God." That is, everything was created from the Word. In the same way, the quality of your creation is determined by how true you are to your word. What you say is more important than any legal document because it sets a selected destiny into motion—it gives the universe consistent instructions about the kind of reality you want to create.

For the Laika, there is nothing more important than being true to one's word, so they're very careful about what they say to themselves and others. They believe that to utter a single negative syllable to someone is to cast a curse, and that to say something positive is to give a blessing. If you were to say to someone, "Are you okay? You're not looking very well today," by the end of the day, she would be ill. Similarly, if you were to remark, "You're looking radiant," even if that person wasn't actually feeling that way, within hours or minutes she would be beaming.

But what if that person really is looking like hell? To be true to your word means that you can't lie to her. What you *can* do is see the aspect of your friend that is always radiant, regardless of what she might be going through that day, and mirror that back to her. You might say, "How are things? Is there anything I can do for you?" Or you could use your words to remind her of her beauty: "I'm always so glad to see you. Your presence is so uplifting." Then your words deliver truth *and* beauty to your friend.

What you repeat to yourself is equally powerful, such as *I'm a loser, I'm not as smart as so-and-so,* or *I'll never find love,* so you must be careful. If your inner thought is *I'm no good,* then you'll damn yourself to failure at whatever you attempt.

Your word is a vow that you make. And the more you live a spiritual life, the more power your word carries and the less leeway you have to fudge. I experienced a funny example of this on a recent trip to India. I stopped in Rishikesh, a holy city along the Ganges, where I was continually pestered by shopkeepers offering me their wares. After a while, to get them to stop hawking their goods, I began telling them that I would come back later. "You promise?" they asked, and I would answer, "Yes, of course." I knew that I had no intention of returning to most of those shops, but my reply seemed to work and buy me a little peace as I walked through the market.

Yet on my return to the United States, I spent the entire first week dreaming that I was trapped in the shopping bazaars of Rishikesh, haggling with the merchants over articles I didn't even want. Although I'd never gone back to the shops, I had to keep my word and revisit them during my dreams!

Living true to your word builds a spiritual power that's essential if you're to dream into being a better world. Without this power, your dreams never acquire form and always end up collapsing just as they're about to bear fruit. Have you ever met someone for whom everything seemed to go right, only to fall apart at the last minute? His relationship crumbles just as he's about to get married; her big business deal always falls through at the 11th hour; or he finds the perfect space to set up his coaching practice and is about to hang up his shingle, only to find that the landlord has changed her mind and won't give him a lease. Because these individuals lack conviction and treat their word as if it doesn't have much power, their plans inevitably fall through.

Rather than trying to strong-arm the universe into complying with your wishes, practice being true to your word, and build up your reserves of personal power. This will allow your dreams to become an unstoppable force that organizes the world the way you instruct it to. When you practice being true to your word, you stop making excuses for yourself—what you say affirms to the universe that you can be counted on.

Misusing Our Word

When we misuse our word, we squander the personal power that we've built up. When we use our voice to blame or create shame or guilt in others, we're practicing the worst kind of offense because we're using what we say to destroy instead of create. It's worse for a father to angrily tell his daughter "You're stupid!" than to beat her with a stick—the physical bruises heal, but the emotional wounds caused by those angry words form a scar that the child will carry for many years.

Misusing our word depletes our personal power, so we can then only daydream. When we lose enough of our power, our reality can only mirror the world around us, causing us to be mired in the collective nightmare of our times.

A prime example of how we misuse the word is gossip, which has become the bread and butter of our culture today. We speak poorly about others behind their backs without thinking much about it, feeling a sense of camaraderie and solidarity with those we gossip with and enjoying that we're "in the club"—that we're okay while others are not.

Our defense of gossip is that it's true: our father-in-law really is a know-it-all, our neighbor is a genuinely awful parent, and that Hollywood actor is a true nut. Yet when we practice integrity, we don't misuse our word in this way. Instead, we allow ourselves to see the know-it-all's insecurity and need to feel smart and important, and we can have compassion for him. We understand that our neighbor isn't malicious, but overwhelmed by stress and frightened that her child will embarrass her or turn out badly. And we realize that we don't know public figures at all.

In other words, we find it in us to be kind and offer gentle help or guidance, knowing that this is more likely to lead to others' healing and growth than treating them with contempt is. We stop ourselves from gossiping and feeling smug because we know that distracts us from seeing our own flaws and addressing them. We recognize these individuals as our teachers and are grateful to them for reminding us that we want to be able to accept others in all their imperfection.

Gossip is a poison that makes us feel right about ourselves at the expense of another. Every time we muckrake, we cast a curse upon our target that will bring misfortune to us and to him. Our words will install an energetic cord to that person, thus ensuring that he or someone like him will be brought into our life in the future.

We get many chances to practice being true to our word when we deal with our families because with them, we do a large part of our emotional growing—first with our parents, then with our spouses, and later with our children. Keeping our word with loved ones is the most difficult as well as the most rewarding challenge, as our children and spouses always hold us accountable. My daughter will say to me, "But Dad, you promised that we would . . . ," and she's almost always right. Then I make myself stop working and take her to whatever activity we had agreed to do. If I can't stop what I'm doing just then, I negotiate for a bit more time. But I don't try to weasel out of my agreement.

I've laid the groundwork for communication with my daughter based on integrity, on being true to my word, and on making sure my word is true. So once in a while, she'll come up and say, "But Dad, you promised . . . ," and burst out laughing because she knows it's not true. Then she'll amend her words to say, "I would love it if we could . . ." We show others through example that integrity is the highest form of spiritual practice, no matter how difficult it might be to maintain at times.

The practice of integrity also requires that we own our mistakes. So often we're embarrassed when we realize that we've goofed, and we try to cover it by projecting the mistake onto someone else. Our minds chatter away, rapidly telling us, "He was so difficult to work with that he made it impossible for me to stick to our agreement," and "If she would have communicated better, I wouldn't have screwed up." We'll always find ourselves involved in conflicts, misunderstandings, and disagreements; however, when we practice integrity, we choose not to get defensive or cast blame and write a story in which we're the victims of someone else's bullying.

When we avoid taking responsibility for our mistakes and try to cover them up with half-truths and outright falsehoods, we weave a tangled web of deceptions that we get lost in. We may even start believing the lies we've told, even if they make no sense. We might destroy our relationships with others and ruin our reputations. But the worst damage is that we waste the personal power we could be using to dream a world of beauty into being.

Owning your mistakes means not just acknowledging them but correcting them and making amends. I'm reminded of a man I know who went door-to-door selling a cure for Dutch elm disease to homeowners back in the late 1960s, when the affliction was ravaging many city trees. My friend really believed in this cure—in fact, when he realized months later that it didn't work after all, he actually went back out and contacted each one of his customers to offer them a refund.

Finally, please note that being true to your word means never *withholding* it. It's extraordinary how many wrongs can be set right with a simple "Forgive me." For many years, I felt awful because my father never said, "I love you." But later in my life, when I understood the terrible cost of not speaking your word, I forgave him and developed compassion toward him. I realized how difficult it must have been for him not to be able to express his feelings.

When we recognize that words have power and the most incidental events can be fraught with meaning, we're ready to go beyond hummingbird to the level of perception in which we don't need to analyze, visualize, or do anything to understand our world or change our dream. When we're at eagle, we experience ourselves in the dream and know that we're the dreamer. We know that although we can change the dream, everything is just as it's supposed to be because we feel ourselves at one with Spirit, whose dream is always perfect exactly as it is.

INSIGHT 4

The Way of the Sage

To be a sage means that when you look around you, you perceive only beauty.

In this chapter, you'll come to understand how everything you experience is a projection of your inner landscape, or dream. This means that nothing ever happens to you and no one ever does anything to you, since you're the creator of each event and incident in your life. So you never need to fix anything in the outer world—if you want to transform some circumstance that appears to be outside of yourself, you just need to own it and change it within.

For the Laika, the world is a screen that we project our movie onto. This doesn't mean that the world isn't real . . . the world is *very* real. We simply confuse the image we project with reality, trying to change the action on the screen when what we really need to do is edit the movie or change the script entirely. Once you understand that you can do this whenever you want, you'll forever cease to be a helpless victim or an innocent bystander.

If your partner says an angry word to you, you'll heal it within. And while you can't change what he said (nothing can—not psychotherapy, nor an angry retort), you *can* change your experience of it. When you're no longer disturbed by your partner's words, he'll be less motivated to project his unhealed parts onto you. Or if you're late to the airport and miss your flight, you can't change that, but you *can* heal it inside of yourself, and then everything will turn out exactly as it should. When you know that you're dreaming up everything that's happening, you can then understand that missing your flight is only part of a larger movie you wrote—even if you're unaware that you did, in fact, pen it yourself.

Just as you don't remember dreaming during the night, you can also forget that you're visualizing while awake. You've probably had times in which you were aware that you were in the middle of a dream, and perhaps you even told yourself that you needed to remember it upon awakening. This is known as *lucid dreaming*. Over millennia, the Earthkeepers developed practices to help them become conscious during their sleep, thus influencing their experiences in the dreamtime. They also developed methods to help them remember that they're dreaming while awake so that they can direct their waking images with more grace and lucidity. You'll learn these disciplines later on in this chapter.

The Role of Conscious Dreaming

We interact with the domain of vibration and light through the practice of *conscious dreaming*. In hummingbird, we pray without using words, perhaps seeing the job we want coming through as we visualize abundance. But when we step into eagle, we don't limit ourselves to the vision of a bowl of rice or a beach house in an attempt to define and control how the prosperity we create manifests—instead, we let the universe take care of the details.

We may want to say a supplicant's prayer, asking God to cure our friend's AIDS or help us get a job soon, but this is not the practice of conscious dreaming. You see, when we dream from the level of eagle, we become one with Spirit, a universal stream that's bigger than we are; yet it is one that we can enter, navigate, and direct in order to bring forth what we desire. We merge with this river of vibration and light, becoming its tides, and the bursts of orange and yellow that are suns not yet born pulsate within us. Then our will and that of Spirit are one, and "may Thy will be done" acquires a new significance. We change our energetic vibration and attract to us and others that which vibrates in a similarly divine manner.

An Earthkeeper practices dreaming by allowing her mind to become silent. Like the surface of a lake that is absolutely still, it reflects everything perfectly. But as soon as a gentle breeze picks up, the surface of the water breaks into ripples, causing the mind to reflect only itself. A Laika is able to still the waters of her mind so that they perfectly reflect the infinite possibilities that exist. Then she can enter the matrix of creation, where she disappears and only Spirit remains.

We, too, can embody prosperity and actually dream it into being. When we become peace, serenity, *and* abundance, these will prevail in our lives.

The World as You Dream It

If you're wondering what it would be like to dream a better world, don't worry—you've probably already experienced this everyday magic at some point. Maybe you were in such a wonderful mood that you smiled at the clerk at the grocery store and observed her mood lift in response to yours. Or perhaps you were able to calm someone who was fearful by just being present and embodying bravery as you sat next to him and held his hand.

When we're at the perspective of eagle, our effect on the world is very great, even if we're unaware of it. We have much more power than we think we have. Remember the theory in physics (which I related earlier in this book) about the butterfly flapping its wings in Beijing and causing a tropical storm in the Indian Ocean? The minuscule change in the atmosphere created by the butterfly's movement can actually result in a significant change in the weather thousands of miles away. So while it's impossible to stop the swirling winds of a tropical storm at the literal level, what if we could find that storm when it's still a whisper on the butterfly's wing? We could stop disasters long before they happen and plant seeds that would yield tremendous fruit.

However, we must keep in mind that if we're able to prevent the butterfly from causing a storm in the Indian Ocean, our action might just spark one in the Caribbean instead. So rather than trying to prevent storms, we recognize that they're a part of nature and we exist in harmony with them. From eagle, we realize that nothing needs to be changed, that everything is perfect as it is, in its own way. Then we're free to change anything we wish because we no longer have an investment in righting some wrong.

Healing the World Within

Imagine that you could change anything on Earth. What would your world be like if anything were possible? Would you end hunger in Africa? Stop the killing of the whales? Bring peace to the Middle East? Whatever you wish to do, it's something you need to heal within you; that is, you must embody healing, peace, abundance, harmony, or whatever quality you desire to experience in the world.

Let's say that you want to save the whales. Well, you don't have to leave your job, your family, and all your responsibilities, board a Greenpeace boat, and stop a whale hunt. In fact, if your passion becomes zealotry, it may be a sign that your intent is not actually to save the whales, so you probably won't get very far in helping them. When your true intent is to heal the wounded creature *within* you, you become blind to how you can actually help those *outside of* you. You become self-righteous and refuse to consider any options that might result in something less than a 100 percent victory. You close yourself off to creative solutions, compromise, and negotiation, and reach a stalemate . . . while the whale hunting continues.

It's much better to address your unhealed nature. Rid yourself of your "inner Ahab," who has become an obsessive predator, and stop "harpooning" others just because you feel that you've been hunted and trapped and someone needs to be punished for it. Whenever your passion is out of sync with your effectiveness, consider whether the discrepancy is a result of your needing to heal a struggle within you, rather than projecting it onto the world. When what's inside you is free, what's outside you can be liberated as well.

The opposite of zealotry, which is rooted in the unhealed parts of ourselves, is apathy. Instead of seeing the possibility of healing within and opening themselves up to dreaming something new, too many people feel overwhelmed and give up. Apathy is rampant in the world today because so many of us have allowed ourselves to fall asleep. I believe that this apathy is a side effect of the collective nightmare that makes us close our eyes, drift off, and ignore the need or suffering of others—along with our own ability to make a difference.

It's our job to co-create reality, partnering with the divine. In the Western story of creation, on the seventh day God finished making the world, and all that was left to do was the naming of the plants and animals. In the story of creation for the Laika, on the seventh day the Great Spirit told the humans, "For I have created the planets, the stars, the butterfly, the eagle, and the whale. Truly, they are things of beauty. Now you finish it." For the Laika, creation is not complete: We have to not only be the stewards of all life, but we must also finish the process of creation. Dreaming the world into being is not only a gift, it's a calling and a responsibility. If we don't answer the call, who will?

Working with the Intelligence of the Universe

There are many wonderful works of fiction about time travel, which are inevitably cautionary tales about what happens when we tinker with events that were meant to be. On some level we know that the universe has its own wisdom, and stopping what we perceive as a disaster might result in another, greater one elsewhere.

The Laika similarly know that we can change just about anything we want in our world, as long as we're willing to take on the karma. At the level of serpent, we try to change things by force; at jaguar, we change things through will; at hummingbird, we change things through visualization; and at eagle, we change things through dreaming. When we're perceiving at the level of serpent, karma seems to catch up very slowly, which is why some people seem to get away with terrible actions with impunity. At jaguar, we experience our karma a bit faster, always within this lifetime. At hummingbird, karma is immediate, so we feel the results of our actions instantaneously: Good deeds yield immediate blessings, and bad actions bring about instant consequences. In eagle, there is no karma, because there is only Spirit and "may Thy will be done."

When you let your ego rule and insist that you must control events, you end up in a constant struggle against the universe. Yet you can choose to simply be with that butterfly in Beijing—not pushing it or willing or visualizing it to do anything other than what it's doing. Your very presence will create balance and healing; and you, the butterfly, the wind, and the storm become one.

It's difficult for us in the West to trust that we can achieve peace and happiness if we're not doing something active to bring it about, but embodying peace and happiness *does* bring it about. Our egos don't want us to believe that we can have infinite power by immersing ourselves in the wisdom of the universe, but it's true.

For example, many young people today are fascinated by witchcraft because they think it might give them a chance to have a greater influence over what happens to them. They want to believe that if they follow a spell's instructions to the letter, they'll be able stop a bully from picking on them, make a popular kid like them, or magically become as physically attractive as a movie star. They don't realize that real magic doesn't come from chanting incantations or mixing together herbs with a mortar and pestle, but from shifting one's perception and embodying confidence and grace. The Laika certainly don't have to wear clothing that indicates their power and position—when they enter a home, food appears without their having to ask for it, and blessings are bestowed without having been requested. Their presence has a radiance that others respond to, and words or symbols of power are unnecessary.

I remember hiking through the Altiplano with don Antonio years ago and arriving at a village where it hadn't rained for many months. The high mountain lagoons, which stored the town's water during the arid summer months, had begun to dry out. When they saw us coming, the villagers greeted us and asked my mentor to call the rains. The old Laika asked for a hut where he could fast and meditate; for four days, he had only water to drink.

I was starting to get concerned when he emerged in the early afternoon of the fourth day. Don Antonio started walking to the edge of the village, to where the mountains began a precipitous drop to the Amazon basin, and told me that he was going to "pray rain." I corrected him, saying he must mean he was going to pray *for* rain, and he said, "No, I am going to pray rain."

He came back two hours later, and there were great big thunderclouds overhead. Within minutes, the rains broke out. All the villagers were dancing with joy and thanking him, but he explained that he had done nothing—it had simply rained.

At that moment, I understood what my teacher had done. He had stepped into eagle, and dissolved. He had ceased to exist for that instant, which was infinite. There was only Spirit there, and thus no one to pray to. He simply prayed rain. And it came.

Later on I asked him why it had taken so long: Did he always need to fast and pray for four days when he wanted to enter the level of eagle? He answered that when we arrived at the village, he noticed that it was out of ayni. It was so out of balance, in fact, that *he* became out of balance, too. He couldn't do anything until he went back into ayni—when he did, so did the village, and the rains came. The old man knew that everything is healed from within.

The Mad Mind and
the Collective Nightmare

When we discover that we're dreaming the world into being, we recognize that we also create the nightmares of our reality. So why do we conjure up poverty and tragedy? The problem is the mind. You see, while our ability to think is extraordinary, and reason and logic are powerful and of great value, the mind itself is crazy. (After years investigating mind-body medicine, I came to the realization that the mind can only create psychosomatic disease, not health. The only way to create psychosomatic health is to shut off the mind completely.)

In fact, the mind doesn't really exist, other than as a figure of speech. Even though there's no scientific evidence for its existence, we dearly want to believe in it and its power because we hope that it holds the key to solving all our crises. This fascination with the mind started after our search for the soul failed. First, during the time of Michelangelo, we looked for the soul in the liver, but it wasn't there. Later, we looked for the soul in the heart . . . then we looked inside the brain . . . and when we weren't able to find it in either place, we settled for the idea of the mind.

In the 1950s, psychological notions of the mind became popular with the rise of *identity theory,* which holds that states and processes of the mind are identical to states and processes of the brain. A machine that performs magnetic resonance imaging (MRI) can show that feelings of compassion are associated with a region of our brain, even as angry thoughts show up in another region. However, in the 1990s, neuroscientist Candace Pert, Ph.D., shared her discovery that the body, not the brain, *is* the subconscious mind, and that it communicates via *neuropeptides,* which are molecules that are produced by every thought we have. Dr. Pert discovered that thoughts have a biochemical component: While thoughts are real, neuropeptides are real, and the brain is real, what we think of as the mind is actually just the ego in disguise.

The Nature of Thoughts

Thoughts are different from ideas: An *idea* is when it occurs to you to go to the store or attend a yoga class, while a *thought* is the incessant brain chatter that's turned on the minute you wake up. Thoughts are often long-winded: *If I go to the store now, I won't have enough time to make my yoga class, and then I know I'll be out of sorts, so maybe I should go to yoga first. . . .* Or a thought may be a judgment: *That yoga class is too hard.*

Unlike ideas, which are fresh and original, thoughts are memories that are triggered by something in the present. For example, if you smell a rose, you're there in the fragrant moment, not pulling yourself back to think about the scent. Yet as soon as you think *rose* or *red,* you're making an association with something you learned, thus removing yourself from the experience. When there is no thought, there is just the scent; when thoughts enter the picture, you lose the moment.

In fact, most of our thoughts are disguised memories of experiences that occurred in the early years of our lives, before we were born, or even in former lifetimes. When we were kids, we placed everything in our mouths and tasted the world. Later we played for hours in the sandbox or with our toys and got lost in daydreams. Then around the age of seven, thoughts began to appear in force: We started to acquire a sense of self and discover where we ended and the world began. We were no longer absorbed in the realm of touch, taste, smell, and feel. Prior to this time, we had no thoughts—we only had experiences. Afterward, our authentic experiences became fewer and fewer until, in our old age, we become haunted by continual thoughts of what once was.

Every thought that rumbles around in your brain is a replay of a drama in which you were the victim, rescuer, or perpetrator. Stop for a moment and listen: What are you thinking of even as you read this book? Remember that thoughts are not original, brilliant, or creative—your instinct, ideas, and ability to dream are.

We find it impossible to think outside the box because thoughts *are* the box. And when we identify with our thoughts, we suffer a case of mistaken identity. I am not my thoughts, I simply have them, in the same way that I'm not my car, my house, or my clothes (although I have those as well). And we know what kind of trouble we get into when we believe that we are our car, our home, or our clothes; and we try to fix a problem by buying Chanel couture or a new set of golf clubs.

Thoughts are like dust that settles on our skin during a long journey, forming a thick crust. After a while we begin to rub a spot raw to get down to our real selves. What we need to do is stop rubbing off the dust in a few places here and there, like we do with therapy, and get out the fire hose to wash it all off. The Laika developed energetic practices that accomplish this in a very short time, by clearing the imprints from our past etched in our luminous energy field. I have described these in detail in my book *Shaman, Healer, Sage,* and I teach them to my students in the Healing the Light Body School as a way to bring rapid transformation to themselves and their clients.

The exercise you performed earlier on healing the way you died in three previous lifetimes (see page 102), will help clear imprints from the LEF. The exercise you will perform next, of discovering the sage, will achieve very powerful results.

EXERCISE: Finding the Sage

Pause for a moment and become aware of how your thoughts appear and disappear, without identifying with them. Close your eyes and observe your thoughts as if they were clouds forming in an empty sky and then dissolving again. Don't chase them or try to stop or control them— simply observe them. Notice how after a few moments you've drifted off onto a chain of thoughts and have forgotten your observation altogether.

Take a deep breath and witness once again the flurry of thoughts that race through the empty sky of your awareness. Don't try to control them, because this is when the mind appears, eager to "solve" all the problems it can. The mind thrives on conflict: When you stop the one within you, the mind disappears, thoughts melt away, and only the sage remains.

The mind is afraid that you'll discover it doesn't exist, and it fiercely wants you to pay attention to it and value it. But once you discover the sage, you'll wash off the dust from a thousand lifetimes and be left with baby-soft skin through which to experience the world. You will have lost your mind and come to your senses.

Not Identifying with Your Thoughts

In many Eastern traditions, the sage is discovered through the practice of meditation. Practitioners spend the first few years of their study sitting on a cushion observing the craziness of the mind, like a bad movie replaying itself over and over again. When *I* sit down to meditate in the morning and all I can focus on is that my back hurts, I let my mind dwell on my sore back. If I try to force my mind back to my breathing, I know I'm in for a frustrating time. What I do is simply identify with the sage, who is observing it all, smiling at how silly everything is. There's no conflict, so the mind gradually dissolves. My back may still hurt, but I don't identify with it, nor do I suffer from it. Thoughts continue to appear and disappear, but my attention resides with the empty sky that is the sage.

When I wish to find the sage, I ask myself these simple questions: "Whose back is sore?" and "Who is it that is asking the question?" And there I am, the sage. You can practice this query with anything you're doing. You can ask, "Who is sitting here meditating?" or "Who is reading this book?" And then, "Who is asking the question?" The ultimate answer will always be the sage.

Once you find the sage, it will show you how everything you believed to be real is a projection. The world is a movie screen, and what's playing is your dream or night-mare. The sage sits on a comfortable chair watching the entire drama unfold. She occasionally gets up to get a cup of tea, knowing that the feature will still be playing when she returns. The question that comes up is how the sage can be so foolish as to think she's the action that's happening on the screen.

Have you ever been so absorbed by a book that you lost track of time and began to feel the lives of the characters inside the pages? Have you ever seen a film that had you in tears or made you so afraid that you had nightmares for days? Well, we've similarly been lulled into a trance by the movie created by society and feel that the action we're see-ing is real. But the sage can change what's on the screen—in fact, she's the only one who can.

The sage fixes everything within, giving the actors new roles, putting on a new reel, or turning off the projec-tor lamp altogether. She finds a spiritual solution to every problem, no matter how difficult and challenging, rather than trying to change things at the physical level.

Once you discover that you are the sage, the madness of the mind takes up only a tiny fraction of your awareness, whereas before, it took up 100 percent of your attention. At this point it becomes easier to reach the perceptual level of eagle—old assumptions dissolve as you look at situations with new eyes. When I practice this with a cli-ent who comes to see me because he has a life-threatening condition, for instance, I no longer perceive fear, danger, or death as the only possibilities; instead, I simply see the opportunity for great healing.

Recognizing How You're
Dreaming the World into Being

When I traveled to Peru for the first time, I was over-whelmed by the poverty and the beggars who would gather around me in the streets. I was so moved by the misery I saw that I would give away all of the change I had on me, and at times even the clothes I was wearing. Then one day a friend suggested that I make a contribution to one of the many charities in Cusco instead. He explained, "Once you no longer see the unhealed parts of yourself in every one of these children, you'll no longer feel obliged to feed every beggar, and they'll leave you alone."

I did what he suggested. I gave a generous donation (which was much more than I could afford at that time) to a Catholic orphanage, and I began to consider the possibility that all the barefoot, runny-nosed kids in the street were parts of me. At first I was heartbroken and distraught; but with time, something shifted. I no longer felt compelled to help everyone I saw, and by and large, the street kids began to leave me alone. My dream changed: As I looked around me, I saw more than just poverty—I began to notice the beauty of the land and people. But first I had to make a contribution to a charity for this realization to happen. After all, those boys and girls still lived in a reality where they had little to eat, and I needed to respond to that.

An Earthkeeper realizes that while you have to change everything within, you still have a responsibility to others and to the planet. The way to modify the dream is to own everything that you perceive is amiss with the world: the ugly, the violent, the beautiful, and the powerful. Perceive every hungry child, violent criminal, rich celebrity, polluted river, and tropical island just as if they were a dream and you were seeing every character, setting, and plot twist.

The mythologist Joseph Campbell once said that what we call reality comprises only those myths and stories we haven't quite seen through yet. Once we do so, we understand that they're just fairy tales. We come to this realization by seeing through the eyes of hummingbird. This is why I found it so easy to be an anthropologist—I could arrive at a village in the upper reaches of the Amazon and be the only one who saw that the emperor has no clothes (in some of the villages I visited, that was literally the case).

We're able to see the dream or nightmare that others are trapped in so much more easily than our own. We quickly perceive that our friend is creating his own misery, but we still think that our own grief is the result of some tragedy that befell us. But when we discover that reality is really a dream, we can wake up from the collective nightmare, and what was hidden before becomes ridiculously apparent. We can see, for example, that we can't meet our spiritual needs by buying a bigger car, that we can't fix our children by changing them, and that progress is not the cure for poverty. So we sell the big car, change ourselves and watch our children change, and understand how poverty is the result of progress and modernity.

I recall sitting across the dinner table from the Indian economist Vandana Shiva as she described how the annual $50 billion in aid given to poor nations by the West is more than offset by the *$500* billion in annual interest payments flowing from developing nations back into the developed world to pay for dams and hydroelectric megaprojects of dubious value. I hardly touched my food as she explained that subsistence farmers in India weren't poor, they simply didn't produce any goods beyond what they consumed—that is, the limits of human consumption were determined by what nature provided. Rather than trying to change the flow of a river to make land in an arid climate produce a bumper crop of the most profitable product, farmers planted what naturally grew well and did not overfarm the land.

Then Western economics introduced the belief that these farmers had to produce more than they consumed in order to create wealth so that they could attain "quality of life." Consequently, Indians left their family land to live in squalor in cities such as New Delhi, and subsistence farming gave way to huge farms and agribusiness. Today, between 250 and 300 million Indians who once farmed on family plots survive on less than one dollar a day; and they don't have clean drinking water, health care, education, or the prospect of a future for their children. Yet we cling to the old dream that if they could just create more wealth or join the march of progress, their problems would magically disappear.

Dreaming a Different World

If the way of the sage is true, then it has to apply not only to our private, personal universe but to the world at large. So how do we dream an entirely different world?

If you see that the butter from New Zealand that's sold at your neighborhood grocery store sells for less money than butter churned upstate by a local farmer, dreaming a different world means recognizing that this doesn't actually mean that the New Zealand butter is cheaper. You know that there's a cost to the environment when trucks, trains, and ships transport the butter long distances; and when you buy butter from far away, you make it very difficult for the local farmer to stay in business, working under quality conditions and overseeing the manufacturing himself. You realize that the real cost of the New Zealand butter is actually higher than that of the locally produced brand.

You dream a different world at the literal level by buying local produce, unplugging the TV, and showing your children how to see through the innumerable advertisements that bombard them. Yet changing your shopping habits isn't enough. You want to intervene not only at the literal level of serpent, but also at the level of Spirit (eagle), where you can step out of time and enter the stream of timelessness and the unknowable.

We've all gathered many bits of information about the world we experience with our senses and recognize that beyond us looms the unknown, but at eagle we recognize that along with the known and the unknown is the *unknowable*. In other words, when you walk the way of the sage, you step beyond the truths you've accepted and begin to enter that which can't be known through the senses, but can only be experienced. Staying in your head and gathering more information won't help you at this stage—you have to take a quantum leap into changing your way of acquiring knowledge. You'll do so through the practices of mastering time, owning your projections, no-mind, and indigenous alchemy.

The Practice of Mastering Time

To master time, you let go of your idea that effect follows cause, and you step into the stream of timelessness.

In the West, we've been taught that time flows in one direction only, that the future is always ahead of us and the past is always behind us. This is *monochronic time,* which flows linearly, going at its petty pace from day to day. But time doesn't just fly like an arrow; it also turns like a wheel. That's why nonlinear time, or *polychronic time,* is considered sacred. Here the future seeps into the present to summon us, and we can change events that have already occurred.

The main operating principle of linear time is causality, or cause and effect, which is the basis of modern science: *This* happens and therefore *that* happens. Causality means that the past is always spilling into and informing the present. We believe that we're a mess today because our parents weren't nurturing enough when we were kids or because we come from a long line of dysfunctional people. But when we perceive time as turning like a wheel, the main operating principle is *synchronicity,* or the serendipitous occurrence of events. What we call coincidence or chance is as important an operating principle as causality is.

The Laika believe that the chance occurrence of events, such as how two people happen to run into each other serendipitously, is just as significant as their cause, or why those two people were in the same place at the same time. Synchronicity allows for future causation and is more interested in the purpose and meaning of an event than in its cause.

I'm reminded here of when poet Robert Bly tells the story of Manolete, one of Spain's most renowned bullfighters. As a boy, Manolete was thin and frail, a fearful child who clung to his mother's apron strings and was terrified of the bullies at his school. Psychologists have explained his calling to fight bulls as a compensatory mechanism—that is, he was trying to prove to himself and others that he was indeed a brave man. But Bly argues that Manolete could have had a foreboding that he would be facing 2,000-pound locomotives in the ring one day, which would have given him every reason to be afraid as a child.

So if time does indeed flow in more than one direction, then the future can be reaching back into the past and beckoning us to it as much as the past is pushing us forward. The reason it does not do so is because we perceive time as linear. The Laika know that the cause of a present event may actually lie in the future. In other words, on the days you hit all the red lights on your way to work, don't start to think that you should have stayed in bed because the universe is conspiring against you and your plans. Instead, recognize that you're operating in sacred time and that the universe is actively conspiring on your behalf. It makes sure that the train leaves three minutes late because you need to get on it, or it makes sure you forget to set the alarm or that you hit every red light because you're not supposed to be on that train.

If we perceive time in this way, we don't become irritated and wonder, *How could I be so stupid as to miss that train? Why do I have such bad luck?* Our stress is reduced tremendously because we trust that both good and bad luck are part of a larger plan.

There's an old Zen story that illustrates this point. A farmer had a horse, but one day it ran away, so the farmer and his son had to plow the fields by hand. Their neighbors said, "Oh, what bad luck that your horse ran away!" The farmer simply replied, "Bad luck, good luck—who knows?"

The next week the horse returned to the farm, bringing a herd of wild horses with him. "What great luck!" exclaimed the neighbors, but the farmer responded, "Good luck, bad luck—who knows?" Then the farmer's son was thrown as he tried to ride one of the wild horses, and he broke his leg. "Ah, such rotten luck," sympathized the neighbors. Again, the farmer responded, "Bad luck, good luck—who knows?"

A few weeks later, the king recruited all the young men into his army to prepare for battle. The son, with his broken leg, was left at home. "What good luck that your son was not forced to go to war!" exclaimed the neighbors. And the farmer remarked, "Good luck, bad luck—who knows?"

The Advantages of Sacred Time

Taking it personally when the world doesn't conform to your expectations causes stress, and studies done at Harvard University have shown that 95 percent of all illnesses are caused or exacerbated by stress. Imagine what can happen to your tension level when you step out of causality and into sacred time. You'll enter a world in which you're never early or late—you simply arrive when you get there, and it happens that everyone else also shows up at the right moment.

Mastery of time doesn't mean that we're unable to keep the commitments we make to show up on time for others; rather, it means that we're in such perfect ayni that we always appear at the right moment. By mastering time, we give the universe the opportunity to do what it does naturally, which is to conspire on our behalf. We let go of the belief that we have to manipulate the world around us and "take charge" in order for life to work out. We discover that from the perspective of eagle, we only need 5 percent of our energy to affect the world in the way we'd like, not 95 percent. That's because we're able to fix things in the future, before they're even born.

Stepping out of linear time also allows us to enter the timeless domain from which the universe is dreaming itself. Within this sacred time, we can find the most desirable destiny for ourselves and choose it. And once we've done so, we can easily change the path we're on.

One of my students had been struggling for years to make time to paint, which she considered to be her calling. But with three young children and a full-time job, she found that she was unable to get to her easel. Moreover, she was reliant on fast food, as she had little time to cook for her family, and she'd put on 30 pounds. The weight gain had affected her self-esteem and she'd lost her confidence. She thought that before she could even pick up a brush, she had to start eating right and exercising . . . but before she could do *that,* she had to transform the spare room that she used for storage into a studio . . . and on and on it went.

While each task my student set for herself initially seemed daunting and insurmountable, after experiencing sacred time, she was able to discover the artist in herself and install it into her future. She found herself beginning to carpool with other mothers, and she felt inspired to buy more wholesome and nutritious foods and cook healthful meals for her family. She forgot about needing to have a studio to paint and set up her easel in the backyard, finding in the process that her time somehow organized itself to support her artist self.

When we practice the mastery of time, we're able to reach the end of the journey we've selected, instead of reaching the one selected for us by statistics. For example, I have clients who have a medical condition and are facing a grim prognosis, as statistics say that they'll most likely die in the same way that others with that condition have. Yet by stepping into sacred time, they're able to track along one of the few destiny lines that leads to a more favorable outcome and install that into their future. After that, they have a better chance of defying the odds and regaining their health, or they enjoy a peaceful and pain-free transition.

Understanding Nonlinear Time

Although we've come to believe that time is a physical reality that moves at a fixed speed, when we practice dreaming, time doesn't have a direction. It doesn't move along a straight line, as when we dream of a long-gone relative and then about our children. And there is no cau-sality: When we dream the world into being, the future doesn't have to build upon the past, and the past doesn't have to predetermine our present.

In sacred time, the future as well as the past is available to us, and everything is happening at once—and we can only dream the world into being from this place of time-lessness. As we raise our perception to that of eagle, we get closer to experiencing this sense of infinity. Rather than waiting for a far-off day in the future when we can recover our original nature and return to Eden, the Earthkeepers say that now is the perfect time to step into infinity and recover our divine self and walk with beauty in the world.

Eternity is an endless sequence of moments; infinity, on the other hand, is a place both prior to and after time, before the big bang and after the universe again collapses. That is, it is outside of time itself. In this place of infin-ity, you can influence events that occurred in the past and nudge destiny. Here, the future is compelling you as much as the past is. You may never know why you missed the train or ran into someone you used to work with as a result, but you're aware that these events have a meaning and even a reason for occurring. You trust that your under-standing will follow your experience instead of preceding it. No matter how confusing or uncomfortable the moment is when you miss that train, you accept and surrender to it, knowing that great things come to those who trust Spirit.

An Earthkeeper understands that if you want to change a situation, you have to start by accepting it as it is. You recognize that this moment is perfect—and then you can change anything you want.

Once you step outside of time into infinity, the past and future disclose themselves to you—you can see tomorrow, and the day after tomorrow, and even the day that you will die. It's important to erase your conscious memory of this so that you can be fully present in the moment each day of your life. You want to wake up saying, "What a beautiful day this is!" instead of "This is the day I'm going to die," "This is exactly one year before the date I'm going to die," or what have you. You don't want to get stuck in time again, perceiving death as a predator and forgetting your original nature. That means that you'll want to keep the secrets you learn in this place of infinity from your ego.

You see, 12 billion years ago, the immense force that we know as God, which existed in an unmanifested void, decided to experience itself. With a big bang, it formed all the matter in our universe, and then it continued to explore itself through myriad forms—from rock to grasshopper to moon to elephant. Yet since the immense force was omnipresent and omniscient, each of its manifestations also possessed these qualities. To know itself through its many forms, it had to keep the nature of its being a secret even from itself.

When we step out of the "arrow of time" and experience infinity, we reclaim our original nature, which is God. When we return into time, we lose that awareness so that we can experience life in our clock-ruled world, which is what we're meant to do. We return to everyday life unaware that we're God and are dreaming everything up. So as we go about our daily lives, the knowledge of our original nature drives us to serve our experiences rather than expecting them to serve us. That is, instead of cooking a meal with the expectation that it will nurture us, we nurture *ourselves* in the preparation and serving of the food, infusing the experience with meaning. We no longer search for meaning in situations, but rather bring meaning and purpose to every encounter; we no longer search for truth or beauty, but rather bring truth and beauty to every situation.

We often expect rituals to be experiences that serve us, making us feel holy, patriotic, proud, connected to others, and so on. Consequently, we're not used to opening ourselves up to the beauty, absurdity, and drama that any given experience might provide. When I was a child, I recall thinking that my first Holy Communion was going to be a deeply transformative experience, as it would fill me with the power and light of the Holy Spirit. But when the priest placed the white, sticky wafer in my mouth, I didn't feel transcendent at all. I didn't understand that it was up to *me* to make the experience profound.

If we keep the knowledge of our omnipresent, omniscient nature at hand, aware of it at every moment, we'll never have to strive for transcendent experiences or enlightenment. We'll know that everything we do is sacred, so we'll no longer search for meaning, truth, beauty, or purpose. We call off the search and bring beauty to every action and truth to every encounter. Having been to that place of timelessness, we'll find it easier to be present in the moment rather than thinking about what we should have done, ought to be doing, or might do later. Whether we're kissing the one we love or sweeping the floor, we lose ourselves in the instant and its complete perfection.

The Practice of Owning Your Projections

To own your projections, you must discover and acknowledge the parts of yourself that you've refused to look at. It turns out that everything you believe to be true about the people around you, or the situations you find yourself in, mirrors a story you hold about the way the universe works. When you understand this, you can take a long, hard look at every difficult situation in your life and then change it within.

What Heisenberg observed about the subatomic world is also true in our dimension—that is, whatever we observe, we alter in the seeing. But to change it, we must first recognize that we're seeing a reflection of our hidden selves in others.

The psychologist Carl Jung called these hidden parts the *shadow,* finding the metaphor valuable to help him understand the unseen aspects of humankind. How aware are you of your physical shadow? Take a moment and look for it right now, on the ground or on the table. It's always there, following you everywhere you go, yet you're seldom aware of it. Sometimes we cast very long shadows, such as when the sun is setting, and sometimes our shadows are small and contained, such as when the sun is overhead. When you own the parts of yourself that make you feel uncomfortable, you no longer hold anyone else responsible for your pain or happiness. Then you shine with your own light, like the sun, which is the only thing that casts no shadow.

Our shadows are those parts of ourselves that make us feel that we're not good enough, that we're unwanted, or that we're a failure and will never be happy; and *projection* is the mechanism through which we cast these undesirable qualities onto others. Individuals have shadows, but groups can have them, too. An example of how an individual can project a negative shadow is when a closeted politician publicly advocates limiting the rights of gay people. Until he heals what he's carrying inside of himself, he'll continue to project his self-hatred onto others. Another example is when someone blames "all the Republicans (or Democrats)" for everything that's wrong with the United States.

An example of a group shadow is the Nazis. In the 1930s, Germany was in a depression, yet many Jews were upwardly mobile, becoming successful scientists, scholars, musicians, and entrepreneurs. The Nazis projected their collective shadow onto the Jews, blaming them for all of their country's problems. They couldn't bear to think that their inability to create great art and thrive economically might be due to their own failings, so they felt that they had to find scapegoats. This was a far more popular option than facing themselves and working on their own shortcomings or their culture's problems. Projection is the mechanism that tells us: "*They* are the problem."

On the other hand, we also cast positive shadows. For example, many people who feel undesirable and have trouble embracing their own beauty project it onto movie stars. They're enthralled by the exquisite creatures on Hollywood's A-list and will even get plastic surgery to try to look as attractive as their idols do. But no amount of surgical cutting or implanting will ever be enough to make them feel beautiful. Marianne Williamson once said that it's not our darkness that we fear the most, it's our light. What she was referring to is how most of us tend to disown our own beauty and tremendous talent, keeping ourselves small and diminished.

You project every aspect of your shadow onto the world, be it positive or negative. And the universe is so fluid that it will arrange itself to accommodate all of your projections and prove you right every time. If you believe that you're powerless, talentless, and unattractive deep inside yourself, then you're going to be proven right. Similarly, if you know without a doubt that there is great poetry, grace, and kindness within you, then the universe will give you the opportunity to bring these attributes forth. This doesn't mean that Hollywood will come rushing to your door or your book will automatically zoom to the top of the best-seller list—but it *does* mean that you'll be able to bring your creativity and talent out into the world.

When you recognize that everything you're experiencing as "not you" is a projection of your shadow, you can change the world by owning your projections. Notice that I haven't mentioned "owning your shadow"—a concept of popular Western psychology. The Laika understand that projection is simply a low form of dreaming and that discovering the mechanism is what's important, so we can employ it to dream in a high way.

Unfortunately, with psychology, the more you own your shadow, the bigger the darkness can get, because you fall back into trying to rewrite the script instead of learning to make a new one. Practice owning your projections instead because when you do, the shadow becomes very small. You can start by turning a story like "My spouse is making me unhappy" into "I am making myself unhappy." Your spouse is simply doing what she does, but she's not making you unhappy—only you can do that. When you own the projection, you stop playing the victim. Of course, this doesn't mean that you have to like behaviors that are unacceptable to you. Your partner still has to work on her communication skills, but your happiness no longer depends on whether or not she does.

Merely owning your projection is not enough, though. If you're to dream the world differently, you have to turn your projection into a story of power and grace, which is called a *journey statement*. For example, you could say, "As I make myself happy, everyone around me mirrors that back to me." In this way, you assert your power over your own happiness and can look within for the resources to do so. This will invite the ever-compliant universe to support you.

Let's say a divorced mother finds out that while her children were with her ex-husband for the weekend, he allowed them to do things she's forbidden them to do. She could own the projection of "My ex is hurting me through my children" by telling herself, "*I* am hurting myself and my children." You see, her ex is no longer doing anything to hurt her—he's simply doing what he does (which is probably the reason she divorced him). She doesn't need to punish her kids for not obeying her while at their father's house.

Next, she can turn the projection into a journey statement, saying, "As I love myself, I am able to love my children fully and teach them how to love." Then her mind won't seize onto the thought that she's being a noble rescuer, protecting her children from her ex, and she'll no longer need to write a story in which her ex-husband is the bad guy. She and the children will be all the happier for it. (Of course she wouldn't tolerate any dangerous or inappropriate behavior, but she no longer needs to declare herself right and her ex wrong.)

Keep in mind that a journey statement is different from an affirmation, which in the above example would be *I love myself, and I love my children fully.* Affirmations work, although they're often a blend of longing and wishful thinking. For instance, this affirmation implies that deep down you don't really love yourself—after all, when you do, you don't need to affirm it.

A journey statement is a command to your subconscious that launches you on a path, telling Spirit what direction you want to go in. It reminds you that the choice and power are yours, and it makes the payoff clear: "As I love myself, I am able to love my children fully." Making such a statement allows the woman in our example to break out of the triangle of the three relationship archetypes: She is no longer the victim of her ex-husband's refusal to parent the way she parents; she is no longer the persecutor who angrily demands that her ex and her children answer to her at all times; and she is no longer the noble rescuer, standing up to her ex in order to protect her children from what she considers his bad parenting.

This insight tells you that you can either have what you want or you can have the reasons why you can't have what you want. You can dwell on the thoughts about what seems to be preventing you from feeling joy, peacefulness, and hope, and spend countless hours in therapy trying to understand this; or you can be joyful, peaceful, and hopeful. When you own the fact that you're dreaming a landscape bereft of peace and joy, you get to choose your state of happiness. When you're caught believing that projection is real, you end up blaming your circumstances for why you don't have what you want.

The following exercise will help you own your projections and turn them into journey statements, allowing you to break free from your stories and dream a different reality.

Exercise: Owning Your Projections

Make a list of three current problems you have, using simple statements that focus on yourself. Be sure to name the situation rather than scripting an entire story around it. Here are some examples:

1. "I can't be happy when there's so much sadness and injustice in the world."

2. "My ex-partner is being so rotten to me."

3. "Everything's going so horribly—no wonder I can hardly bring myself to face another day."

Now own the projection and explore the consequences of the thoughts, beliefs, and actions you've chosen. Rephrase your problem in this form: "*When* I do such and such, *this* is what happens." Please note that this exercise is not about assigning blame and feeling poorly about yourself—the purpose is to recognize that you're dreaming your reality and that you can choose to dream a different one. Although the instructions are very clear, you might find it difficult to understand, because the ego is reluctant to go along with this exercise.

Here are examples of owning your projections:

1. "When I only see sadness and injustice in my life, I make myself unhappy."

2. "When I'm rotten to myself, I hurt myself and my ex."

3. "When I dread facing the day, everything goes poorly."

After you own your projections, turn them into journey statements, which reflect your deliberate choices about what you will think, believe, and do. State the results you hope to achieve. Use the form "As I do such and such, this positive outcome results." For example:

1. "As I see the joy and justice around me, I bring happiness to myself and others."

2. "As I live and practice peace, I share peace with my ex-partner and others."

3. "As I arise each new day and greet it with gusto, life beckons to me and all goes well."

Once you've owned your projections, you'll realize that if you could change the external circumstances you imagined were necessary for your happiness, you still wouldn't be satisfied. At the literal level, you can never have enough of what you want because nothing outside of you can fill an internal void. Getting a better apartment, changing your ex-partner, earning a promotion, or attracting a wealthy lover isn't going to make you feel happy and content for more than a short while.

Unfortunately, most of us are so attached to our stories that we'd prefer to conjure up reasons for why we *can't* have what we want. We simply refuse to own the projections—for example, if we can't find a romantic partner, we tell ourselves that it's because there's no one out there who's right for us. We write a story in which we can't find love because we're damaged or are the victim of extraordinarily bad luck.

It can be easier to hold on to the belief that we must be in a partnership in order to be genuinely happy, or to stay attached to our role as a noble rescuer and decide that we can't have peace until we resolve a social problem that has plagued people for generations. Yet when we refuse to own our projections, we miss the peace, the joy, and the abundance of energy, creativity, and enthusiasm that would help us make a real dent in the problem.

When you own the projections and turn them into a journey statement, you realize that you've been dreaming the world into being all along and that you can wake up from the popular nightmare and into the sacred dream.

The Practice of No-mind

When the mind starts to busy itself crafting a story about how we've been wronged, or daydreaming about what our lives could be like if we could only find the right person or situation, we need to extinguish it. Earthkeepers do this through the practice of "no-mind."

Practicing no-mind requires you to break free of your thoughts and get in touch with the sage within, who is beyond thoughts. You don't have to spend hours upon hours in meditation to do this, although the practice can help anyone who wants to master it. When you become aware of how your mind foolishly jumps from thought to thought like a monkey, you can sit quietly, amused by its activity. The parade of thoughts will continue, but you won't get caught up in it. There will only be the sage.

Thus, you'll be able to say, "There goes my mind, obsessing about how it believes I was wronged. That's how my mind acts up when I'm feeling like a victim." And then, a few moments later, you'll forget that you're the sage, and you'll once again identify with the gymnastics of your mind. Then you'll remember and inquire, "Who is it that was wronged?" and "Who is asking the question?"

You make the switch from identifying with the chatter to becoming the sage by asking questions such as "Who is hurt?" "Who is angry?" and "Who is late to the office?" What brings you home to the sage is always this: "Who is it that is asking the question?" The minute you ask yourself this, you break the trance and the mind dissolves. Only Spirit remains, because Spirit *is* the sage.

The chatter in our minds will only stop when the mind is extinguished. Until then, we can simply observe our thoughts, be amused by our "monkey mind," and not identify with it. One day we'll recognize that our genuine self, the sage, resides in the middle of the storm and is unaffected by all the commotion surrounding us—such as the fight with our spouse, the car breaking down, or the stomach ulcer acting up. And then the chaos around us subsides because we realize that it's only a mirror of what's going on in our minds. Slowly but unstoppably, the sage prevails, as the screen of our reality becomes a blank canvas for us to create and dream in.

You can't "make up your mind" to step back and become the sage because once you do, the mind will vanish . . . and it knows it. So in order to protect itself, the mind will tangle you up in all of the reasons why you can't do this practice. That's why you can only discover the sage by inquiring, "Who is it that is asking the question?"—or by ingesting powerful mind-altering substances. Under the influence of these hallucinogens, the mind dissolves, the ego melts away, and all that remains is Spirit tracking itself. However, these plants must only be used under the guidance of a master shaman so that one doesn't become sidetracked or deluded by the experience. Otherwise, they can cause great harm.

I remember the first time I used the legendary *ayahuasca* in the Amazon. When you drink of this potion, you lose all sense of the ordinary self that identifies with your job, your roles, your family, and even your history. The following is a transcription of one of my first experiences with the ayahuasca, which appears in my book *Dance of the Four Winds* (written with Erik Jendresen):

I am moving. And breathing.

I move through a many-layered collage of wet leaves, hanging vines, reds, yellows, greens washed gray by moonlight. My head hangs low to the ground. Faster, I pant. The ground yields slightly beneath the pads of my . . . hands and feet? They move in cadence with the throbbing in my chest. My breath is hot and humid; my heart beats too fast, and I can smell myself beyond the moist tangle of the jungle.

There is a clearing, and there am I, sitting cross-legged, naked, and shining wet in the moonlight. My head is thrown back and my throat is taut, exposed. Arms thrown out lax to my sides, hands palms up on the soil.

I watch myself from the edge of the jungle, still but for my breathing. Behind me, the jungle stirs sleeplessly.

I move with the lithesomeness of a shadow, following the contours of the clearing's edge to circle my prey.

Soundlessly. Closer.

Now we are breathing together. My head falls forward. My chin touches my chest. I raise my head, open my eyes to stare into yellow cat eyes, my eyes, animal eyes. A half-breath catches in my throat, and I reach out and touch the face of the jungle cat.

After many years of meditation, and after a decade of training with the medicine plants of the Amazon, I discovered that I didn't need external devices to discover the sage that has always existed. He was there before my body was born; after all, I am not my body—I only inhabit it—and the sage will be there long after my body returns to the earth.

The following exercise will help you to discover, or rediscover, the sage inside of you.

EXERCISE: The Query

Sit comfortably in your favorite chair and dim the lights in the room. Light a candle if you wish, but make sure that you're in an absolutely quiet place because you want to listen to the chatter of your mind. Close your eyes and begin to take deep, regular breaths . . . count your breaths from one to ten, and then start at one again.

After a few minutes, you may notice that you're counting up to 27 or 35, as the mind becomes absorbed with what you need to do later in the evening, what you failed to do at work, or how upset you are with someone. Or perhaps there's a tune playing inside your head (once while at a meditation retreat, I had the Beatles' "Yellow Submarine" stuck in my head for an entire week!).

Bring yourself back to counting your breaths. Now ask yourself, "Who is angry?" "Who is late?" "Who is breathing?" and then, "Who is it that is asking the question?" Be still, and observe what happens when you ask this.

Try to make this query regularly throughout the day, even if you're not sitting in meditation. The more the sage rises to the forefront of your awareness, the longer she'll remain in residence. The sage will shift you out of your serpent awareness into eagle so that you become conscious of the great blank canvas of creation, along with your power to dream it into a world of beauty and grace.

The Practice of Indigenous Alchemy

To practice indigenous alchemy, we follow a four-step process for transcending our roles and our situations.

The alchemy of the Europeans had to do with placing dead matter such as sulphur and lead into a crucible, applying fire to it, and hoping to transform these substances into gold. The alchemy of the Earthkeepers was different: They placed living matter into the crucible of the earth and allowed the fire of the sun to warm it, thus growing corn, the living gold. The indigenous Americans were a practical people who bred and crossbred their wisdom with their corn. That's why we say that you "have to grow corn" with all you say and do; otherwise, you're engaging in useless talk and activity and will remain stuck in roles and situations, learning nothing and growing nothing.

The Laika are keen observers of nature who take notice of how the beehive and the anthill behave like a single organism with many independent parts. They observe how ants farm fungus in their hollows, and how bees manage to communicate the location of flowers to each other through an intricate aerial dance. They understand that the survival needs of a bee can best be met at a higher level by the hive, and the well-being of an ant can best be assured by its colony. To the Earthkeepers, the beehive and ant colony are simply examples of the indigenous alchemy, of how life seeks higher levels of order and complexity by creating these collective beings we know as anthills and beehives.

Similarly, the problems of cells (such as the need for food and warmth) are best solved at a higher level by tissues, the requirements of tissues are best solved by organs such as the stomach and heart, and the needs of organs are best addressed by a living, breathing creature. In other words, the eagle's cells need nourishment, but an eagle is a more effective hunter for food than its stomach or cells are.

When a Laika wants to solve a problem, she practices indigenous alchemy and then works her way up to a higher level of perception, where solutions are readily available. She solves the problems of cells from the level of eagle (or of bees at the level of the hive).

To learn indigenous alchemy, we must understand the interconnectedness of the great hive of humanity, and of all life. Claude Lévi-Strauss, the renowned anthropologist, once said that for us to comprehend the workings of the universe, we first have to understand how a blade of grass works, turning light into life through photosynthesis. But for a Laika to figure out the workings of a blade of grass, she first has to grasp the workings of the universe. Indigenous alchemy helps us achieve this.

Indigenous alchemy is made up of four steps: *identification, differentiation, integration,* and *transcendence.* Identification is the quality of serpent; differentiation, of jaguar; integration, of hummingbird; and transcendence, of eagle. Cells can be identified as single organisms, yet they differentiate (specialize) into muscle cells, brain cells, skin cells, and others; then they integrate into heart, stomach, brain, and the like; and then they transcend the sum of their parts. You can't describe an eagle by its organs, yet they are what it's made up of.

The philosopher Ken Wilber explains this process and describes how as children, we identify with our parents, and then as adolescents, we pull away from Mom and Dad in order to differentiate and develop our own identity. Eventually, we're able to integrate our parents into our lives without fearing that we'll lose our sense of self, and we finally transcend by becoming parents ourselves. (Of course some people will not literally become parents, but will mentor and nurture other people.) We all know people whose parents passed away before they had the opportunity to integrate their relationship to them, and what a terrible thing this is.

We're always in the process of identifying with some things, differentiating from or integrating with others, and transcending others. I love to watch the shifts that occur over the course of the football (soccer) season, for instance, as rabid fans identify with their regional teams and despise the opposition. Yet when a team is selected to represent their country in the World Cup, the fans start cheering for players they despised weeks earlier, now identifying at a national level.

This is similar to the way that most people in the United States identify with some region (such as the Midwest), but differentiate from people in another region (for example, the Southeast), yet when a crisis such as terrorism occurs, we integrate and all identify as Americans. In the final step of transcendence, we identify ourselves as Earth's citizens and understand that certain issues like global warming, AIDS, polio, and others can only be resolved at the level of the planet. Our loyalties to the needs of our region and our country are superseded by our loyalty to all our fellow humans and the earth.

Indigenous alchemy not only describes the four levels of perception, it also allows you to navigate through them. It not only explains that water is H_2O, it also teaches you how to make it rain. Indigenous alchemy is the fast track to transforming your life . . . but you can't skip any of the steps of the process. After all, cells can't become eagles, unless they differentiate into organs and integrate into systems first.

◈

One of my students has a daughter who's an avid soccer player, and my student spent hours every week shuttling kids to games in her minivan. Everyone considered her a soccer mom, but she knew that she was meant to be a teacher and healer, for she felt that she had a very strong spiritual calling. One day she discovered a lump in her breast and was diagnosed with cancer. In everyone else's eyes, she was now a soccer mom and a cancer patient. However, she didn't want to identify with her disease—she wanted to differentiate from it and then overcome it. It was then that she signed up for our Healing the Light Body School.

After the first weeklong training session, she announced to her family that she was neither a soccer mom nor a cancer patient—she was a healer—but no one else believed her. "I am not my cancer," she would tell her fellow students, "I am simply fighting cancer." *We* believed her, and respected that she was differentiating from the disease. Soon she began to achieve integration, saying, "I am not my cancer, and I'm not fighting it, I'm learning from it. It's my wake-up call." Integrating her cancer allowed her to reach the final step in indigenous alchemy, transcendence. By the end of her training, she was able to say, "My cancer saved my life by allowing me to reinvent myself."

My student had ceased identifying with her diagnosis; instead, she recognized that her healing had to do with honoring her calling and enlisting the support of her family in helping her become the healer she wanted to become. She had to go through chemotherapy and transform her personal relationships. She couldn't take any shortcuts and become a healer overnight because it wouldn't have been authentic. It wouldn't have resulted in her own transformation, only in a flight of fantasy. The process of indigenous alchemy takes time.

Breaking out of the serpent state is the most difficult step, because when we identify with something—such as being a mom, recovering alcoholic, cancer patient, or child of abusive parents—we convince ourselves that this is who we really are, and we become trapped in the nightmare. We forget that *we're the one* dreaming it all into being. Fortunately, each of the levels in indigenous alchemy makes us gradually more conscious so that we can transform the dream.

Now, understanding that the needs of acorns are best solved by oaks is something that occurs at the level of jaguar (the mind). To transform ourselves, we have to go beyond understanding what it is we want to change—we have to experience the transformation at the levels of hummingbird and eagle. When an acorn is placed in the earth, it must let go of its identity as "seed" and begin to think of itself as "oak." So, too, must we let go of our perceptions of ourselves as being bogged down by a problem or trapped in a role, and envision ourselves as free from what we are identifying with or clinging to, regardless of how unlikely it seems that we'll be able to achieve that.

The following exercise will help you change at the mythic and energetic levels. I've used it with myself, with my clients, and when I've been called upon to consult with organizations. Read it through; think about the problems you're facing in your life; and begin to gather stones, sticks, and other objects to represent those problems and roles. You may want to start by writing out what you want to differentiate, integrate, transcend, and identify with, and then think about these changes.

Review the Owning Your Projections exercise that appeared earlier in this chapter (see page 184) if you've forgotten how to transform your projections into journey statements. When you're ready, you can perform this exercise to make changes at the level of hummingbird or even eagle.

EXERCISE: Transformation
Through Indigenous Alchemy

This exercise is best done outdoors, on a beach or in a yard, using a stick to sketch out a circle on the ground. You're going to create four *mandalas,* or three-dimensional representations of your prayers; so if you can, perform this practice in a place of power, a natural earth temple such as a hollow near a river, or a sacred place in the woods or mountains. You can also do it in your living room using four sheets of paper.

1. First draw a four-foot circle around you as you stand in place. This is the **serpent ring.** Next, select a stone or a stick to represent one thing you're identified with. An easy way to find this out is to think of any issue you're dealing with right now—if it's a problem, you've identified with it. Concentrate on this issue while holding the stone in your hand, and then blow into the stone all that you feel about this problem: your concern, your anger, your frustration, and your hurt.

Place the stone anywhere you like inside the circle. You can do this with up to three issues that you're grappling with at this time, arranging them inside the circle any way you wish. You can label the stones with a marker, or just remember that the little jagged white stone represents being underemployed, the dark stone with mica chips is the one you're using to represent being a self-sacrificing Catholic woman, and so on. (Alternatively, you can map on a piece of paper what each stone represents.) Decorate your circle, using seaweed, leaves, earth, moss, and anything else you like to represent the swirls of energy and people that are around this problem, influencing it.

2. Draw another circle next to the first one, where you'll place an issue or theme that you've differentiated from. This is the **jaguar ring.** For example, you may no longer identify with being a Catholic, with the city of your birth, or with being a businessman. Select recent examples—perhaps something that really preoccupied you last year has now resolved itself or is no longer looming menacingly over you. But maybe a few years ago you were a very vocal feminist, and although you remain true to these values, *feminist* no longer describes who you are.

Blow the feelings you have about these into another stone or stick, and arrange it inside your mandala. Again, you can do this with one and as many as three themes, but keep in mind that using more than three themes at a time can become confusing. Decorate your circle with moss, grass, and sticks to represent the people and energy who surround and influence what you used to be.

3. Now draw another circle next to this one, where you'll place one element that you've integrated. This is the **hummingbird ring.** For example, you may have integrated being an elder, so you're not looking for new gray hairs in the mirror every morning or worrying about your age anymore. You may have integrated being a writer or a healer, so you no longer need to hide it from others or have to explain yourself to people who you feel may judge you wrongly.

For example, for many years I was embarrassed to let people know that I was a shaman, so when the person seated next to me on the airplane would ask what I did, I would answer that I was a medical anthropologist. Now I'm comfortable with my role as a shaman and healer, and have integrated this aspect of my life. And although I still don't actively strike up a conversation with those sitting next to me on a plane, when I do, they're generally very interested in the topic. Destiny now seats me next to people who will mirror back to me my integrated self.

4. Now draw a final circle, where you will place one element that you've transcended. This is the **eagle ring.** You may have transcended your nationality, for instance, and now consider yourself a citizen of the world. Or if you're familiar with the music and literature currently popular with people younger or older than you are, you may have transcended your generation. You might also have transcended your social status; being rich or poor; your role as son, daughter, or mother; or even a physical ailment or diagnosis. Blow one of these elements into a stone or a stick and place it inside your circle.

Once you've created these four mandalas, you have a map of the core themes of your life, the issues that are on your plate. But a map is only useful if it allows you to navigate through the territory it describes, so select one stone or stick from any one of the circles so that you can use indigenous alchemy to transform the issue it represents.

Let's say that you want to start with something from the differentiation (jaguar) circle—in this case, the role of daughter, represented by one of your stones there. Retrieve that rock, and hold it in your hand for a few minutes. Examine the cracks and crevices in the stone as you recall your previous identification with the role of "daughter," and then think about the period of rebellion you went through when you didn't speak to your mother or when you had to prove her wrong. This rebellious period is what allowed you to differentiate from this role, even though it may have caused a lot of pain and grief to everyone involved.

Think about how you blamed your mother and held her responsible for your unhappiness . . . and now own the projection. Say aloud, "Being the daughter of my mother is not what made me unhappy. I made myself unhappy and could not be who I really am," and notice if this statement rings true for you. Owning the projection allows you to completely differentiate—that is, to realize, "This is not me any longer."

Next, turn the projection into a journey statement. It could be something like, "As I am true to who I really am, I become happy and can share this with my mother and others." The journey statement is what takes you from the ring of jaguar to that of hummingbird, of integration. The journey statement contains the lessons you need to learn in order to integrate "daughter" into a higher level.

The important thing here is the lesson. Once you "get" it and are ready to take on the journey statement, you can bring the stone to the circle of hummingbird. You've embarked on the sacred journey without spending two years in therapy or pondering whether you have big enough wings or adequate time or energy. The lesson might be that you have to forgive your mother—and yourself—as both a mother and a daughter. (Note that the lesson will be different for each one of us.) When you learn the lesson, you can move on.

As you can see, the way out of identification (into jaguar) is by owning the projection. The way out of differentiation (into hummingbird) is by turning it into a journey statement and asking yourself, "What do I have to learn in order to move on?" The way beyond integration into transcendence (eagle) is to see opportunity where you once saw only problems. Indigenous alchemy allows you to do your learning within, rather than through your children, parents, spouse, and co-workers. Of course you then take the lessons with you into the world by calling your mother and asking her to forgive you, or by telling her you love her. You no longer need others to mirror back to you the lessons that you haven't learned yet.

An Earthkeeper can perform the process of alchemy using her medicine pouch, which is a collection of stones and sacred objects she carries with her. She uses a stone or object to represent each theme that she's working through in her life—when she has learned the lessons and is able to move the stone into the next ring, that object can go into her bag as part of her spirit medicine, and it can be of benefit to others. When she's ready to transform the issue at the next level, she can bring the stones out of her medicine pouch. (The stones are only a representation, a visual aid, as the alchemy happens within.)

Eventually, the Earthkeeper's medicine bag contains all the wisdom about herself and nature that she has acquired. Her stones have become objects of power, and her identity is then based on that which she has transcended. She sees opportunity everywhere, and is able to say, "The mountains am I, the red-rock canyon walls am I, Spirit am I."

Try it yourself. . . .

AFTERWORD

The Laika have always been ordinary men and women who live extraordinary lives. They weren't born with special gifts from Spirit, but acquired uncommon grace and power through the practice of the four insights. Some grew to be renowned leaders and healers, while others lived quietly, raising their children and growing corn. And the insights were never forced upon the next generation—the Laika felt that people would come to them when they were ready and felt a calling to do so.

Many of you who read this book will receive such a calling from Spirit and will long to make a difference in the world and in your life. When you come to the path of the Earthkeepers with sincere intention and an open heart, you'll soon notice that you're not alone. You'll find yourself in the company of like-minded individuals who strive to live by ethics and vision. You will also be guided by the luminous ones who lived on this planet many thousands of years ago—beings who are now part of the great matrix of life. These Earthkeepers will add their power and vision to yours.

As you step into the stillness of hummingbird, you'll feel the presence and sense the wisdom of those who have broken out of linear time and now dwell in sacred time, in infinity, free from the grip of karma and rebirth. When you've risen to a level of vibration where they can attune to you, and your luminous energy field (LEF) has been scoured clean of the psychic sludge left by past traumas, the Earthkeepers will come to you and guide you. When you connect with them, you'll be able to recall stories that you never experienced directly but that are now yours. You'll remember sitting around a fire with the buffalo behind you and meditating in a stone temple above the snow line.

Since the Earthkeepers come from the future as well, they can help us access who we're becoming as humans 10,000 years from now. The memories from the past are available to the Laika, who tap in to that vast reservoir of knowledge that exists outside of time. The visions of the future appear as possibilities, since everything yet to come is still in potential form. That's why Earthkeepers from the Hopi, Maya, Inka, and many other tribes gather regularly to pray peace on the planet. They do so by tracking along the possible futures for Earth to find one in which the rivers and the air are clean and people live in harmony with each other and nature. The act of finding this desirable future installs it into our collective destiny and makes it a little bit more probable than it was before, because it has acquired another quantum of energy from these shamans.

When we connect with the luminous ones, their stories become ours: We actually "remember" making our way across the Bering Strait or crossing the Sonoran Desert into Central America, or even before that, making our way over the Himalayas to the fertile green valleys on our great journey north from India. When we partner with the Earth-keepers from the future, we have knowledge available that can upgrade the quality of our DNA. This runs contrary to scientific wisdom, which says that our genes can only be informed by the past, by the gifts and illnesses our ancestors had. The Laika understand that when we're free of the bounds of time, the future can reach backward like a giant hand to pull us forward. We can be influenced by who we're becoming.

As you practice the four insights I've detailed in this book, your chakras will become clear and you'll acquire what the Laika know as the "rainbow body." This is when your energy centers glow with their original radiance because they're not dulled by illness or trauma. Remember that each of your chakras has a color, and when they're shining with their original light, they emit the colors of the rainbow. When they're dulled by trauma, your LEF acquires a grayish hue and your chakras become pools of psychic sewage.

Once you acquire a rainbow body, the luminous Earth-keepers can reach out to you because they recognize that you share a common vision and calling. When this happens, and if you've developed the ability to see into the invisible world, you can discern the former physical forms of these luminous beings. (Sometimes people will perceive the ancient ones as Native American elders, wearing robes from Asia, furs from Siberia, or feathers from the Amazon.) This happens at the level of serpent. At the level of jaguar, you'll be able to perceive their thoughts and feelings. But the most interesting phenomenon begins to happen at the level of hummingbird, where you have access to the Earthkeepers' wisdom and stories. And then, at eagle, you can "download" a new and better version of the "software" that informs the LEF, which will then inform your DNA, giving it instructions on how to create a new body that will age, heal, and die differently.

There's nothing you need to do to attract the luminous ones—they'll come to you when you invite them to do so and are ready to receive them. (Remember that when the student is ready, the master appears.) They will not disturb you in any way, but are available to support you in your efforts to bring a bit more light and healing into the world. They're also there to protect you from the negativity and fearful energies on the planet today.

The Nature of the Luminous Beings

The Earthkeepers are our medicine lineage, for they're humans who rose to the level of angels. Some are in bodies, some are in spirit form, but all have a mandate to protect those who are looking after the well-being of the planet. The Buddhists call these beings *bodhisattvas*—they are the finest spiritual allies anyone can have, and they provide us with knowledge on how to become angels ourselves. This is what the prophecies of the Laika mean when they tell us that we have the potential to become *Homo luminous*. We can develop the luminous energy fields of angels within our lifetime, and the insights offer us the keys to do so.

When we practice the ways of the hero, luminous warrior, seer, and sage and evolve to *Homo luminous*, we no longer have to call on angels and archangels to help us find a parking spot or our fortunes because we're becoming like them. Remember that in the Bible, God said, "Behold, the man is become as one of us, to know good and evil: and now, lest he put forth his hand, and take also of the tree of life, and eat, and live for ever."

As we become Earthkeepers, we join the ranks of the angels, who come from many different worlds and were the original souls present after the Creation. They don't cycle through bodies as we do because they don't need a corporeal form, as they don't need to learn and grow during an existence in the material world. They have everlasting life, and they are the keepers of many worlds in many galaxies.

The practices of the four insights are vitally important when one sets out to become an Earthkeeper. When we practice nonviolence, peace, and integrity, we don't become food for others, and we're able to maintain the wholeness of our LEF. Our spiritual power isn't squandered and remains available to us for our growth.

Initiation Rites

The training of the Laika revolves around the insights—but the Earthkeeper's training also has an energetic component, or a series of nine initiations, that accompanies them.

These nine rites of passage can help us develop a new architecture in our LEF, for they anchor each of the critical junctures in the process of becoming *Homo luminous*. The rites are the sum total of attunements that we go through as we transit from the body of a human to that of an angel. First given to ancient teachers by the archangels themselves, these nine steps are now passed on from teacher to student. When an Earthkeeper performs these rites on a pupil, it's the Laika lineage that transmits itself, leaping from the head of the master to the student as they lean into each other and touch, forehead to forehead. To transmit this rite, the Earthkeeper simply maintains sacred space and embodies the vibration of the level she wants to transmit.

I would like to share the nine rites with you briefly so that you can be aware of them. When you undergo these initiations, they are yours to transfer to others as you please. Remember that these rites of passage can still be received directly from Earthkeepers in the Spirit world. If you open yourself to the process, you will experience these initiations in the dreamtime. But if you have the opportunity, do try to receive them in person. (Please visit my Website, **www. thefourwinds.com,** for the name of someone in your area who is qualified to give these rites.)

The Nine Rites

1. The first rite consists of **protections installed in your LEF.** Known as the "bands of power," these are five luminous belts representing earth, air, fire, water, and pure light. They act as filters, breaking down any negative energies that come your way into one of the five elements so that these energies can feed you instead of making you toxic or ill. Since these bands of power are always operating, negative energies bounce right off them. In a world filled with fear, these bands provide essential protection.

2. The second is **Healer Rite,** which connects you to a lineage of shamans from the past who come to assist you in your personal healing. The Laika know that we all have tremendous spiritual assistance available to us, and these

beings work on us during our sleep to heal the wounds of the past and of our ancestors.

3. The third is the **Harmony Rite**, in which a Laika transmits seven archetypes into your chakras. In the first, you receive the archetype of serpent; jaguar goes into the second; hummingbird into the third; and eagle into the fourth. Then three "archangels" go into your upper three chakras: Huascar, the keeper of the lower world and the unconscious, is transmitted into the throat (fifth chakra); Quetzalcoatl, the feathered serpent God of the Americas and keeper of the middle world (our waking world), goes into the sixth; and Pachakuti, the protector of the upper world (our superconscious) and keeper of the time to come, goes into the seventh chakra.

These archetypes are transmitted into your energy centers as seeds. These seeds are germinated with fire, so you have to perform a number of fire meditations to awaken them and make them grow. Afterward, they help combust the psychic sludge that has built up in your chakras so that they can shine with their original light, as you acquire a rainbow body.

This practice helps you shed your past the way a snake sheds her skin.

4. Next is the **Seer Rite**, which is performed by extending pathways of light between the visual cortex in the back of your head and your third-eye and heart chakras. This practice awakens your ability to perceive the invisible world. Many of our students at the Healing the Light Body School find that after a few months of performing the Seer rite, they're able to perceive the world of energy around them.

5. The fifth is the **Daykeeper Rite.** The Daykeepers were the masters of the ancient stone altars found in sacred places throughout the world, from Stonehenge to Machu Picchu. The Daykeeper is able to call on the power of these ancient altars to heal and bring balance to the world. This rite is an energetic transmission that connects you to a lineage of master shamans from the past.

According to lore, the Daykeepers called on the sun to rise each morning and set each evening, to make sure that humans were in harmony with mother earth, and to honor the ways of the feminine. The Daykeepers were the mid-wives who attended births and deaths, as well as being the herbalists, or *curanderas*. They were knowledgeable about the ways of the feminine earth. This rite helps you begin to heal your inner feminine and to step beyond fear and practice peace.

6. Next comes the **Wisdomkeeper Rite.** Lore says that the ancient wisdom resides in the high mountains. These ice-covered peaks in the Andes were revered as places of power, just as other mountains around the world—from Mount Sinai to Mount Fuji to Mount Olympus—have been honored as areas where the human meets the divine.

The lineage of Wisdomkeepers are medicine men and women who defeated death and stepped outside of time. The job of the Wisdomkeeper is to protect the medicine teachings and share them with others when appropriate, so this rite will help you step outside of time and taste infinity.

7. The seventh is the **Earthkeeper Rite.** This rite connects you to a lineage of archangels, which are guardians of our galaxy, reputed to have human form and be as tall as trees.

The Earthkeepers, who are stewards of all life on Earth, come under the direct protection of these archangels and can summon their power whenever they need to in order to bring healing and balance to any situation. The rite of the Earthkeepers helps you learn the ways of the seer and dream the world into being.

8. Then comes the **Starkeeper Rite.** This rite anchors you safely to the time after the great change that is said will occur on or around the year 2012. According to lore, when you receive this rite, your physical body begins to evolve into that of *Homo luminous*—the aging process is slowed down, and you become resistant to diseases you were once vulnerable to.

After I received these rites, I noticed that I no longer processed events primarily at the level of serpent. When I caught a cold, for example, I processed it at the energetic level and it would wash through me in a day or two instead of a week. I started to live and process the events that occurred in my life at the level of hummingbird and eagle. When *you* receive these rites, you'll acquire stewardship of the time to come and of all future generations.

9. Finally there is the **God Rite.** When you receive this, you awaken the God-light within and acquire stewardship for all of creation, from the smallest grain of sand to the largest cluster of galaxies in the universe. This rite has never been available before on the planet, but it is available today. Although there have been individuals who attained this level of initiation and awakened their Christ or Buddha consciousness, it was never possible to transmit this from one person to another until recently. So while Spirit-to-human transmission happened on occasion, human-to-human transmission was heretofore impossible.

While these rites were traditionally gifted from the Laika to an individual, as you practice the insights, you'll find that you receive these initiations directly from Spirit . . . you'll be touched and blessed by angels. You simply need to open yourself up to the wisdom of the Earthkeepers, and all will be bestowed upon you.

I have seen this happen with my students. They may come for the rites on the evening I'm offering them and be totally unprepared to receive them. They might be distracted or thinking about a problem or concern, for instance, causing them to not be fully present for the experience. And since the transmissions take place in less than a minute, when they realize how unprepared they were, it's too late. Over the next few months, I then tend to observe that they receive the transmission directly from Spirit. I can tell because there is a different valence and quality to their LEF. I can tell that they've been touched by the angel of life.

And so will you.

A NOTE FROM
THE AUTHOR

———————————————— ▄▙▄ ————————————————

According to lore, the wisdom teachings of the Earth-keepers go back more than 100,000 years. During this time, the teachings have gone through many transformations, as mountain peoples migrated to lush farmland and then crossed the ice in Siberia into the thick forests of the American continent. Today, we're going through another evolution as we bring this ancient body of knowledge into the 21st century. And although the outer form of the teachings change, the inner form remains the same.

I believe that we're the new Earthkeepers—after all, it is said that they will come from the West. I would love to hear about your experiences with the insights, along with the success and challenges that you encounter in your practice.

In Spirit,

Alberto Villoldo, Ph.D.
www.thefourwinds.com
villoldo@thefourwinds.com

ACKNOWLEDGMENTS

The real creators of this book are the medicine men and women of the Americas. These individuals lived (and, in many cases, lost) their lives through the courage of their convictions and their experience of Spirit and the divine. These were my teacher's teachers, and I am in their debt for the knowledge that they so graciously shared with me in the 25 years that I trained with the Laika.

I would like to thank Reid Tracy at Hay House for the opportunity to publish this work, along with his trust and encouragement, without which this effort would have been impossible.

I owe my gratitude and thanks to my editor, Nancy Peske, for her inspired hand and faultless pen. She has been a beacon of light in the difficult process of putting these ancient ideas to paper. And my editors at Hay House, Jill Kramer and Shannon Littrell, were stewards of this project from the beginning.

It would be difficult to thank all the people who supported this book through their love and intention, yet foremost among them are Marcela Lobos; Susan Reiner; Ed and Annette Burke, who provided a retreat where I could write by the sea; and the Inka of Peru, whose ancestors walked and taught the wisdom of the four insights.

Finally, I want to thank our students at The Four Winds Society for embracing these insights and bringing the medicine teachings into the 21st century.

ABOUT ALBERTO VILLOLDO

Alberto Villoldo, Ph.D., a psychologist and medical anthropologist, has studied the healing practices of the Amazon and Inka shamans for more than 25 years. While at San Francisco State University, he founded the Biological Self-Regulation Laboratory to study how the mind creates psychosomatic health and disease.

Villoldo directs The Four Winds Society, where he trains individuals throughout the world in the practice of energy medicine and soul retrieval. His Healing the Light Body School has centers in New England; California; the U.K.; the Netherlands; and Park City, Utah.

An avid skier, hiker, and mountaineer, Villoldo leads annual expeditions to the Amazon and the Andes to work with the wisdom teachers of the Americas.

◇◇◇◇